**DAVID WALKER**

*Photography by Richard Goulding*

# jiu jitsu for all
## YELLOW BELT TO GREEN BELT

First published 2008 by
A&C Black Publishers Ltd
38 Soho Square, London W1D 3HB

www.acblack.com

Copyright © 2008 David Walker

ISBN 9780713683462

A CIP catalogue record for this book is available from the British Library.

Note: It is always the responsibility of the individual to assess his or her own fitness
capability before participating in any training activity. Whilst every effort has been made
to ensure the content of this book is as technically accurate as possible, neither the
author nor the publishers can accept responsibility for any injury or loss sustained as a
result of the use of this material.

Typeset in 9.5/13.75pt MetaPlusNormal by Fakenham Photosetting Ltd, Fakenham, Norfolk
Text and cover design by James Watson
Textual and cover photographs © Richard Goulding

This book is produced using paper that is made from wood grown in managed sustainable
forests. It is natural, renewable and recyclable. The logging and manufacturing processes
conform to the environmental regulations of the country of origin.

Printed and bound in China

# jiu jitsu for all
## YELLOW BELT TO GREEN BELT

# Contents

Acknowledgements                                   7
Foreword                                           9
1  Introduction                                    13
   A basic history of Jiu Jitsu                     14
   Martial arts in the 21st century –
   myths and reality                               15
   Anyone can do Jiu Jitsu                         19
   Preparing to train                              20
   Getting in close                                32
   Thinking about weapons                          32
2  YELLOW BELT                                     35
   Traditional techniques                          43
   Self-defence                                    64
3  ORANGE BELT                                     85
   Traditional techniques                          85
   Self-defence                                    102
   Introducing weapons defences                    117
4  GREEN BELT                                      123
   Traditional techniques                          123
   Self-defence                                    145
5  THE NEXT STEPS                                  169
   Glossary                                        170
   Index                                           174

# ACKNOWLEDGEMENTS

My first thanks must go to Richard Goulding, not only for taking all the photographs in this book but also for spending a lot of time considering how to convey the movement and meaning in each of the shots. Jiu Jitsu is a movement-based martial art and it is not easy to capture its essence in static photographs. I'd also like to give a really big thanks to all the Jiu Jitsuka who gave of their own free time to act as 'models' for each of the shoots, and for having the patience and grace to wait while we considered how to illustrate each of the moves.

All of the true stories in this book are from real Jiu Jitsuka – when I asked for written input from Jiu Jitsuka I was overwhelmed by the response. Although not all of the stories made it into the book, I owe a debt of gratitude to everyone who submitted a story for consideration.

Studio III Clinical Services, where I work, are also due a big thanks for allowing me the time I needed to complete the book. Thanks are also due to Gareth Horgan and David Barret Hague at the Jitsu Foundation for the administrative help they gave me and for covering the travel and accommodation expenses of all my 'models'.

In Jiu Jitsu I'd like to thank Steve Allison, Andy McDonnell and John Hamer for all the support and challenges they've given me over the last 25 years.

Ruth, Alex and Charlotte at A&C Black have been brilliant.

Lastly – and they are only last because they have always been there, putting up with me when I was burning the midnight oil or being patient when I had to spend yet another weekend on the book – the biggest thankyou goes to my wife Ingrid and my children Maddy, Jake and Toby. Without them, this book would never have happened.

# FOREWORD

I started Jiu Jitsu by accident. In the early 1970s, I'd tried judo and karate but decided that they and martial arts in general just weren't for me. But meeting two remarkable men in 1979 changed all that.

My first encounter with Peter Farrar could have been my last. In my late teens I'd become pretty rebellious to the point of confrontational. I'd left my music paper in a café and when I went back to get it I found Peter just about to start the crossword. Aggressively, I wrenched it from him. He just looked at me, smiled, apologised and wished me luck in finishing the crossword. I remember feeling totally disarmed. I felt completely embarrassed a few days later when he knocked on my door and asked me if I wanted to join a Jiu Jitsu club.

'Who's running it then?' I asked.

'Me,' he replied.

I couldn't say no. I thought I'd give it a few weeks and slowly disappear off the scene. But from that time until his tragically early death in 1997 Peter was to be my mentor in Jiu Jitsu.

The second remarkable man was Brian Graham, Peter's sensei. Within a year of meeting Peter I was about to do my first grading. The Jiu Jitsu club had arranged a weekend training event with a local martial arts academy; Brian Graham was to teach Jiu Jitsu on one day and run the grading for the club the next.

I really wasn't prepared for my first meeting with Brian Graham – respectful, small, constantly cracking jokes and, like Peter, unassuming. My admiration for him grew immeasurably after one of the other martial artists – a black belt from another discipline – issued a half joking challenge to Brian in front of a group of novices. We were practising wrist locks and the challenge was made, 'Come on mate there's no way that would work against a real punch.'

Brian, smiling, asked the black belt to hit him as hard as he could. Five seconds later the black belt sat on the mat nursing a very sore wrist and his injured pride.

'Now don't forget to call me sensei next time,' said Brian, still smiling. I was hooked.

There are several different approaches or ryu in Jiu Jitsu but all share a very similar history. As you progress in Jiu Jitsu don't just confine yourself to one particular school – you will find that many have a lot to offer. As you will see as you progress through the books, there are many contributions from real Jiu Jitsuka to give you a good idea about what Jiu Jitsu is all about.

A big thank you to all the contributors for allowing me to include your stories and thoughts in the books. The approaches described in this book are based on the Shorinji Kan style of Jiu Jitsu, based on traditional Japanese Jiu Jitsu, but developed by Brian Graham and Peter Farrar through their work with the Jitsu Foundation.

These books are dedicated to the memory of Brian and Peter.

David Walker

# CHAPTER **ONE** introduction

Ju (Jiu) –*(lit)* gentle, soft or flexible

Jitsu – the art or technique

Starting a martial art can be quite daunting, but as a novice you will not be expected to know everything. Above all, remember that even an instructor was a novice once.

Some people who train in Jiu Jitsu would have you believe that you have to be super fit, need to train obsessively, develop muscles where you

**IF THIS IS WHAT YOU WANT ...**

Contestant A had a match with B in the heavy-weight category that went horribly wrong. A threw several intentional kicks to B's groin, and the match went from sports Jiu Jitsu, with a few rules, to a real fight, with the two men trying to kill each other. The men were pulled apart by the referee, trainers and corner men, and A was thrown out of the Association. The Association had their last competition nine days later as many of the Jiu Jitsuka were unhappy under the selfish leadership of their Association Leader, but didn't have the organisation to keep it alive without their leader.

The second incarnation of Association started in November. A was asked to rejoin despite his previous complete loss of control. In December in front of 1500 spectators, A (once again) intentionally and illegally kicked Jiu Jitsuka C in the face, breaking three bones. A was suspended again, and then thrown out of the Association. In April of the following year A and three other senior sports Jiu Jitsuka formed the new Association. This Association began to thrive with the addition of new sports Jiu Jitsuka drawn in by the no-holds-barred approach to the fighting. Large audiences started to turn up regularly to watch the fighting but the Association was still beset by internal feuding over promotions money, while the competitions themselves often degenerated into bloodbaths. On 1st December, the Association president suspended all the sports Jiu Jitsuka after a 'fighting show' that had resulted in several serious and two life threatening injuries, and disbanded the promotion.

**... then you've bought the wrong book!**

never knew they could exist and take part in hour-long wrestling bouts while tying your opponent up in 20 different locks and hitting them over the head at the same time. This book will prove otherwise. If you were fit enough to walk to the bookshop to buy this book then you are almost certainly fit enough to start Jiu Jitsu!

Jiu Jitsu is, above all, a practical, defensive martial art that is fun to learn. At the centre is the key idea that aggression can be overcome by *not* confronting it head on. Instead, you can use your attacker's strength, size and momentum to your advantage; you can use physical distraction or you can focus your strengths on the most vulnerable parts of the attacker's body. By the time you have got to grips with Jiu Jitsu you will be using all of these approaches at the same time.

Because Jiu Jitsu does not rely on strength, people of all ages, shapes and sizes can become very good; training is gradual but always moves forward. As you progress you will learn to defend yourself against increasingly difficult unarmed and armed attacks, using a system of throws, locks and strikes.

I won't lie and say that learning Jiu Jitsu will be easy or quick, although you will quickly grasp a few very effective defences. Your training will almost certainly be imporved by having a willing partner or, better still, by joining a club. Initially you will need commitment, enthusiasm and a fair amount of dedication. When we start turning techniques into practical applications you will

have to be sure that you are totally committed if you are going to be effective.

But this is only half the story. Jiu Jitsu is also about learning to work co-operatively, about developing a real sense of honour, respect and self worth, and of being able to find fun, enjoyment and personal satisfaction through learning. Mastery of all the skills of Jiu Jitsu will take a lifetime. To become proficient in the skills and techniques in these books may not require a total mastery but it will need a lot of dedication.

In self-defence Jiu Jitsu is not about competition; there are no real rules, no right or wrong techniques, simply ones that work and that depend on you – your height, weight, strength, speed, skill level, fitness and, above all, total commitment. The old saying that discretion is the better part of valour holds true in much of Jiu Jitsu. If you don't need to fight then don't, but if you do need to fight then make sure you put absolutely everything into it. In training you work together, learning from each other and working co-operatively. In reality you are alone, applying everything you learned in practice with one simple addition – survival is everything.

## A basic history of Jiu Jitsu

You will be introduced to a more detailed history of Jiu Jitsu in later books but basically Jiu Jitsu was originally developed for use on the battlefield. Many years ago the Samurai warriors of feudal Japan learned a variety of fighting skills that together became known as Bushido – the way of the warrior. Among their many skills they learned how to shoot arrows on horseback, to use katana and wakazashi and to defend themselves when they had lost their weapons or had to fight at close quarters. Over the years, the close quarter skills and techniques they learned were refined into the systems of what we now call Jiu Jitsu.

Literally, Jiu Jitsu is the technique or art of suppleness, flexibility and gentleness although it often doesn't feel very gentle. Judo founder Jigaro Kano, himself a master of Jiu Jitsu who developed Judo from Jiu Jitsu, traced the art's emergence to the period between 1600 and 1650. Records show us that in the golden age of Jiu Jitsu, from the late 17th to mid 19th century, more than 700 Jiu Jitsu systems appeared in Japan. But the history of Jiu Jitsu is long and complicated and no-one is completely sure of its true roots. Many schools were very secretive and focused on specific aspects of training such as the use of pressure points or locking techniques. Since the 17th century there have been many attempts to describe, categorise and classify all the techniques of Jiu Jitsu but this has proved an almost impossible task. Jiu Jitsu is a dynamic martial art that is constantly evolving to meet the needs and demands of the times and environments in which it is taught. Similar techniques are often taught in very different ways but they will all in some way include kicking, striking, kneeing, throwing, joint locking, holding as well as the use of certain weapons.

For the Samurai the only concern in Jiu Jitsu was effectiveness in combat. Methods were tested in duels and public competitions among members of various schools. These encounters were frequently lethal. Such testing not only involved weapons and ways of disarming them but also mortal combat. Samurai often established fearsome reputations through surviving these tests. When we look at pictures of Samurai training we can see many of the techniques that we use today although obviously we don't test ourselves in mortal combat!

Historically, much of Jiu Jitsu was combative but not competitive. This has changed quite dramatically over the last few years with some schools of Jiu Jitsu now focusing almost exclusively on the sports side of Jiu Jitsu and often ignoring the practical self-defence aspects. Other styles such as Brazilian Jiu Jitsu have featured heavily and have had much success in the competitive mixed martial arts forums such as the Ultimate Fighting Championships (UFC) and cage fighting. For those of you who have heard about Jiu Jitsu through sports Jiu Jitsu with its emphasis on competition and ground fighting you will find this book especially useful for exploring the roots and practical applications of many of the techniques you now use in competition.

# Martial arts in the 21st century – myths and reality

Martial arts at their most simple are systems of training for combat. Some of these systems may be old and very traditional, some may be very new; most are based on old systems revised and refined for today. Some martial arts are studied for various reasons apart from just combat skills – these include fitness, self-defence, sport, self awareness, self confidence and mental discipline. Jiu Jitsu incorporates all these aspects.

## SUPERHUMAN FEATS

There is a great diversity of martial arts throughout the world but in general they share a common goal: to defeat a person physically or to defend oneself from physical threat. There is also a deep sense of spirituality within some martial arts and each style has different facets that make them unique. Some martial arts and martial artists may appear to be extraordinary – super-human martial artists performing superhuman feats. The brilliant Wushu monks perform acts that are well beyond the range of most human beings, including martial artists of other styles, but the reality is that the monks have trained for many years in specific martial arts skills that train the body and mind in specific ways. Given the time, training and a huge amount of dedication most of us could learn these skills.

## MARTIAL ARTS AND THE MOVIES

Once you've started Jiu Jitsu you have started to learn a martial art and nowhere in the world is there so much made of the almost mystical and mythical nature of what you are starting to learn than in martial arts movies. When most people think of martial arts films they will think of actors like Bruce Lee, Jackie Chan, Jean Claude van Damme and Steven Seagal, all accomplished martial artists but actors first and foremost. Films like *Crouching Dragon, Hidden Dragon*, *Rush Hour* or even *Casino Royale* may have spectacular martial arts scenes but they are films often totally removed from real life. The choice of technique in a film fight scene is not normally based on the practical, but on the spectacular – the more eye-catching the scene, the more successful it is. It is not intended to demonstrate the useful and simple self-defence techniques that would work on the street. In films, the hero or heroine wins because that is the way it is written in the script. Whether or not they can actually fight or even do a martial art is entirely beside the point.

## PEOPLE GET HURT

In real life, fighting to protect yourself is an altogether different proposition from what happens in the movies. In real life most people are severely wounded or die when they are shot and they bleed when they are stabbed. Learning a martial art will give you an advantage but it will not necessarily prevent you from being hurt. You may well get battered and bruised, the techniques you use may not look very pretty but pretty does not always lead to effectiveness. In the dojo (training hall) you may focus on the aesthetic qualities of the techniques, especially at an advanced level, but you must never lose sight of the fact that before you develop the aesthetic qualities of the technique you have to be certain that you can get them to work in real life situations. The techniques you learn in the dojo will almost certainly look very different when you use them for real.

## ANYTHING GOES? MARTIAL ARTS AND THE LAW

> 'Martial arts give you an edge; they do not make you invulnerable.'

self-defence strategies form the basis of many martial arts and in the 1980s some martial arts tried to update themselves by combining traditional martial arts experiences and techniques with the techniques, strategies and tactics used by the police and military. Many schools of self-defence also started to teach theoretical strategies aimed at avoiding or defusing physical confrontations based on questionable strategies that didn't sit well with the assertive and 'win at all costs' (within what is legally allowed) philosophy of many martial arts, especially Jiu Jitsu.

In real life having to physically defend yourself should be generally thought of as your last line of defence, although there will be some situations where seizing the initiative or provoking an attacker so that you can take control away from them may be your only option. Using the physical part of a martial art can be counter-productive – at the very least martial arts are hard work and you might not be good enough to do what you are trying to do. Even if you are quite capable of looking after yourself, it is still often best to avoid being in a situation of having to physically defend yourself because of possible:

- injury to yourself;
- revenge from the attacker, perhaps not just directed on you but also on your friends and family;
- a sudden escalation in the situation when the attacker is only partially dealt with and suddenly produces a weapon;
- suddenly finding out that your attacker has several friends who you also have to defend yourself against;
- legal reasons.

## MARTIAL ARTS AS SELF-DEFENCE

Although all martial artists would agree that when physical action has to be taken it has to be totally effective, most honest and intelligent martial arts instructors will tell you it is normally better to use techniques to avoid or diffuse trouble before it gets physical. It makes sense to:

## THE LAW AND MARTIAL ARTS

Everybody is allowed to use reasonable force to defend themselves but there is considerable debate among individuals as to what constitutes an acceptable level of physical force. Martial artists do not have to declare their skills before they defend themselves. Some martial arts instructors may teach a limited number of responses to attackers, while other instructors may advocate any means of self-defence up to and including deadly force, such as turning the attacker's weapons on the attacker. In martial art terms, reasonable or acceptable force is that which is required to prevent the attacker from carrying out further violent actions so it is highly unlikely that stabbing your attacker would be seen as reasonable if you had the opportunity to immobilise them more safely or even run away. Laws vary from country to country as to the level of force acceptable for defending yourself from an attacker. A responsible martial arts instructor will teach students to respond with the force necessary to defend themselves based on the situation and not to go totally over the top, in case they find themselves in serious legal trouble.

- stay in groups at night;

- park in well-lit areas;

- avoid excess consumption of alcohol or drugs which could make you intoxicated, vulnerable and unable to fully control your responses;

- try not to attract too much attention from potential attackers;

- don't hang out with violent people you can't trust;

- don't attend parties or other gatherings (especially where alcohol and/or drugs are being heavily consumed) where there are people (especially groups) you don't know and/or can't trust, who could become violent.

Much Jiu Jitsu is based on common sense so if you do have to defend yourself in a real life situation don't use unnecessarily violent language, make threats or get into an obvious fighting or self-defence stance because:

- a potential attacker may seize upon this as a legal excuse for attacking, even if they know there is no real threat;

- an intoxicated or generally violent person may perceive this as a genuine attack or threat and attack you preemptively.

If you recognise that an attack is imminent, you do have some choices before you have to fall back on your Jiu Jitsu self-defence skills.

- Escape by running or driving away, if possible.

- Attract attention from others who may be able to help defend you or frighten or distract attackers, by:

  - yelling or screaming

  - using a personal alarm

  - calling the police on an emergency line

  - putting a physical barrier between yourself and your attacker.

## GETTING REAL

However, sometimes when you've exhausted every other option there isn't a viable alternative to protecting yourself physically. In Jiu Jitsu an important aspect of self-defence training is teaching techniques as close to the real life situations in which they occur. This can be done through role play where one person plays the role of the defender, and one (or more) people will have the role of the attackers. As the defender becomes more proficient, the physical and psychological intensity of the training increases, as does the likelihood of real injury during the training. Some martial arts such as Jiu Jitsu make considerable use of this approach while other martial arts hardly ever use these training approaches.

## Anyone can do Jiu Jitsu

Let's face it, the majority of martial artists are men. Looking at websites and martial arts magazines you'd be forgiven for thinking that not only are most martial artists men but strong, competitive muscular men at that – not the sort of person that you would want to defend yourself against in real life. Fortunately most martial artists have learned one very important lesson, namely that it is far more important to finish a fight than start it. The chances of having to defend yourself against another martial artist are fortunately very low.

There is always someone bigger, stronger, faster, fitter than us, but Jiu Jitsu encourages each individual to make the most of their strengths and overcome their weaknesses. It is not about producing fighters, rather it is about building confidence and helping Jiu Jitsuka to be as good as they can be. Almost anyone can do Jiu Jitsu as it's based on the principal of using an attacker's energy to their disadvantage. Strength and speed are important and do make a difference but they are no more important than skill and sense.

Almost all Jiu Jitsu techniques are designed to exploit the vulnerability of your attacker. This means you have to be physically and psychologically in control of yourself. The more control you have of yourself, then the more control you have of your own body, and the more able you are to use your own control to control others. In Jiu Jitsu you learn how to be physically assertive from a position of confidence and self control, rather

**TRUE STORY: HOW JIU JITSU HELPED ME IN REAL LIFE**

The first way is a very silly little thing but it made me laugh. A few weeks after starting Jiu Jitsu I tripped over something in the street and went flying! This is quite normal for me – I have always been clumsy. This time though, I found myself automatically break falling and did not hurt myself at all. A first – someone getting fewer bruises through practising Jiu Jitsu!

I have been doing Jiu Jitsu for about two months and last weekend I vaulted over a fence without even thinking about it. I cannot possibly explain how amazing it is to feel strong, and to experience the progression as strength develops. Women are not really encouraged to develop physical strength and Jitsu is great for that physically and mentally. The best thing about Jiu Jitsu is my fellow practitioners. I don't know whether it is just because we have a wonderful club but I especially enjoy the intimacy of it all. Jitsu seems to be about trust – trusting in others' competence and trust in physical intimacy with those around you. There is not much of this in the rest of life and I think it is a wonderful thing. You get lots of hugs from your friends – with flying through the air at the end of it – brilliant!!!

**Ryanne**

irrespective of age, culture, sexuality, sex, level of ability or physique, can work together as partners and train as equals so that physicality and assertiveness no longer become identified with something that's bad, scary, or even intimidating.

Fundamentally, Jiu Jitsu is as much about confidence and control as it is about physical movement as for many Jiu Jitsuka the knowledge that they can respond appropriately to physical danger if and when the need arises gives them the skills they need.

## Preparing to train

This book covers the basic techniques you will need to progress through from novice to green belt in Jiu Jitsu. The book is most useful if you are already training in Jiu Jitsu and is no substitute for proper training. To begin with, many of these techniques will feel strange and you will need to practise them many times before they begin to feel natural. It will be normal to make mistakes. Just stop and start again.

Before you start there are some fundamental ideas that will follow you throughout Jiu Jitsu.

- Always respect what you're doing and those you practise with. Jiu Jitsu is potentially dangerous and there is absolutely no excuse for losing your temper or intentionally injuring or humiliating either the person you are training or yourself. If you are experiencing problems of any kind, stop.

than from a mind-set based on fear, hate and anger. To gain this level of confidence and control Jiu Jitsu is generally taught in a non-threatening, supportive environment where all Jiu Jitsuka,

- If you're very unfit or have got a potentially dangerous medical condition get yourself checked out by a doctor first.

- If you are very unfit start exercising before you start Jiu Jitsu. It can be physically demanding and you will get bumps and bruises. If you are unfit but healthy then Jiu Jitsu will help your fitness right from the start but don't push yourself to do anything that you know your body is not ready for.

- Whatever you are practising start slowly and build up speed. There is a difference between technique and application and you need to get the technique right first. Once you know it is right, build up speed until the technique becomes second nature. Jiu Jitsu is done best when you don't even think about what to do – you just do it. Constant repetition leads to muscle memory and the ability to act intuitively and instinctively.

- Jiu Jitsu is as much a mind game – in practice care about your training partner; in real life don't care about your attacker – you don't mind because they don't matter.

- Jiu Jitsu can sometimes feel like a brutal and very energetic game of physical chess where you try to outwit your opponent physically and mentally. In practice learn from your mistakes and constantly analyse what you are doing. Asking for feedback from your instructor or training partners is a sign of confidence, not weakness. In practice getting things wrong is OK; indeed, it will give you a much better chance of getting things right in real life.

- Jiu Jitsu is a full contact martial art so get used to physical contact and be prepared for physical contact when you train – don't be afraid to have a bit of a gentle wrestle even from the beginning. Feel how other people's bodies move in response to pulling and pushing, always look for potential signs of weakness, try to identify openings.

So you've found the Jiu Jitsu club you're looking for and after watching a session from the side have decided that Jiu Jitsu is for you. You walk into the **dojo** – training hall – for the first time, ready for your first session. Good luck!

## WHAT TO WEAR

You can start your first Jiu Jitsu session just wearing track suit bottoms and a tee-shirt; you won't need anything on your feet. Most **Jiu Jitsuka** – students of Jiu Jitsu – wear a **keikogi**, usually referred to simply as a gi, which can either be a standard judo gi or something slightly lighter. Although different styles sometimes have different coloured gi, the most common colour is white. Very light gi, such as those used in karate, are not really suitable as they are easily torn or damaged during groundwork, ground-fighting or when using certain throws. When you start Jiu Jitsu you will almost certainly wear a white belt

21

even if you are a grade in another martial art. This is not to disrespect the martial art you are already doing but simply to signify you are a beginner in Jiu Jitsu. From a safety point of view alone this will protect you from being asked to do more than you are capable of doing. If you have already done another martial art then you may well find that this really helps your Jiu Jitsu. Some Jiu Jitsu techniques may be very similar to ones you have already done and to begin with you may make quicker progress than other beginners.

## DOJO ETIQUETTE

As soon as the **tatami** – mats to absorb the impact of your falls – are laid down, the room in which you train becomes a dojo and there is an expectation on every Jiu Jitsuka that they will follow the dojo rules. Above all the dojo is a place in which you train and respect those you train with in the understanding that Jiu Jitsu can be dangerous and it is as much your responsibility as everybody else's to train safely. Although each dojo will have its own rules, these following general rules will apply to every dojo:

- footwear must not be worn on the mat;
- bow on entry and exit to the dojo;
- no smoking, drinking, swearing, or inappropriate behaviour; treat the dojo as if it is someone's house and you are a guest;

- shoes or zori should be worn when not on the mat;
- clean feet;
- short finger and toe nails;
- clean gi and remove jewellery;
- all Jiu Jitsuka must ask for permission before stepping onto the mat;
- all Jiu Jitsuka must ask the sensei or highest grade for permission to leave the mat and dojo.

The most important rule involves responding to the command **yamae** – stop or halt. There is always a good reason why your sensei will shout yamae and it is normally to do with mat safety. Whenever you hear it, stop immediately and wait for further instructions.

As you enter the dojo it's customary to **rei** (bow) towards the middle of the dojo. The rei is the name given to the traditional Japanese bow or salutation, similar to the western shaking hands. The bow should be performed correctly. The standing bow is performed with feet together, bending forwards at the waist with alignment of neck and back; hands move down the front of the legs until the body forms a 45-degree angle. Always maintain eye contact with the Jiu Jitsuka you are rei-ing to.

When you step on or off the tatami you should rei to the highest grade currently on the mat or the middle of the mat if it is empty.

## TRUE STORY: OVERCOMING FEAR THROUGH JITSU

I have a visual impairment called Stargardt's disease (a form of macular degeneration), which I have had since I was seven. As a result of my poor vision I have always been nervous and insecure when meeting new people and in new situations. Joining the University of Chester Jiu Jitsu club has enabled me to develop confidence in my abilities. Through continued exposure to new techniques, situations and drills I have overcome my fears compounded by my lack of vision and as a result live a much richer and fuller life. Jitsu is not a miracle cure but rather a set of tools that can be used not only for self-defence but for self development.

Howard

At the beginning and end of each session you will be asked to line up to face your **sensei** – all instructors are referred to as sensei. The sensei calls out **kiba dachi** – horse riding stance; **su dachi** – standing with feet together; and **suwari** or **seiza** – kneeling position. The highest student grade will call out **sensei ni rei** – bow to sensei, and the Jiu Jitsuka will rei to their sensei. The sensei, then calls **otagi ni rei** – I return the bow, and reis to the Jiu Jitsuka. Although the kneeling bow is more formal and some Jiu Jitsuka may choose not to rei for religious reasons, in Jiu Jitsu the rei is a mark of mutual respect and not one of compliance or supplication.

## WHO'S WHO

Although this will not apply to all Jiu Jitsu dojo, the next thing you will notice as you step into the dojo for the first time is that many of the Jiu Jitsuka will be wearing different coloured belts. The coloured belts signify what grade the Jiu Jitsuka has attained. The coloured belts are known as **kyu** grades and black belts as **dan** grade.

Many styles of Jiu Jitsu, including the Jitsu Foundation, use modern kyu grade systems as opposed to the traditional white belt (novice) and black belt (competent) system that is used in other martial arts. As a result, any instructor visiting a club at which they do not train or teach regularly can gauge the level of competence of those they are about to instruct, and choose techniques at a level appropriate to the grades present.

The Jitsu Foundation has eight coloured belts and the first two grades, 7th and 6th kyu, contain sub grades called mons which signify how well the Jiu Jitsuka did in the grading – a pass (no mons), a good pass (1 mon), an excellent pass (2 mon) or an exceptional pass (3 mon).

The full kyu grade system is:

8th kyu: white belt (novice)
7th kyu: yellow belt (with 0–3 orange mons)
6th kyu: orange belt (with 0–3 green mons)
5th kyu: green belt
4th kyu: purple belt
3rd kyu: light blue belt

2nd kyu: dark blue belt
1st kyu: brown belt

You will see that some of the brown belts also wear hakama – long black skirt-like trousers – to show that they also teach.

There is a wide variation in the number of different black belt or **dan** grades in Jiu Jitsu. Some styles only have one while others have up to ten. Drawing comparisons between the dan grades in different styles of Jiu Jitsu can be very difficult and sometimes quite pointless as a ni dan – second dan – in one style may have actually trained longer and harder and have more experience than a rokudan – sixth dan – in another style.

The Jitsu Foundation places emphasis on learning through teaching and has a six-level black belt grading system with three dan grades awarded through skills-based gradings and three teaching levels awarded through observation, assessment of teaching skills and the ability to motivate and bring out the best in Jiu Jitsuka.

## THE USE OF JAPANESE IN JIU JITSU

One of the main things that you will notice as soon as you start training is that some of the instructions are given in Japanese and many of the techniques are first identified by their Japanese and then their English name. This shouldn't be too surprising as Jiu Jitsu is a Japanese martial art, and so it's quite natural that you will hear a lot of Japanese terms.

Although there is no practical benefit in knowing a technique's Japanese name and its English translation outside the dojo, the use of some Japanese terms is a reminder to Jiu Jitsuka and their sensei that many aspects of the art they practise are rooted in the discipline and honour of the Samurai. Using Japanese terminology helps maintain tangible links to our heritage.

## HOW MUCH TRAINING?

One of the questions you are bound to ask as you prepare to start Jiu Jitsu will be 'How much training do I need to do?' There's no easy answer to this. A typical Jiu Jitsu training session lasts two hours and Jiu Jitsuka normally practise two or three times a week. Each session starts with a selection of aerobic and anaerobic warm-up exercises lasting about 25 minutes – the aim of the warm up is always to help you reach a state at which you are fit to train, not too tired to train. Although your fitness will improve as you begin to train more, warm ups should never leave you unable to continue with the actual session. If you think you will be able to handle this training regime and have the time, then go for it. If not then don't worry – just do as much as you can manage. You will find yourself doing more as your body becomes accustomed to training in Jiu Jitsu.

At a lower level, training is geared towards improving fitness, working on movement and speed, and learning the basic techniques that underpin much of Jiu Jitsu. As you progress you

## WHY JAPANESE?

Using Japanese gives Jiu Jitsuka pride in undertaking such an ancient art as they are constantly reminded of where it came from and how long it has been developing. But it can also help to give a deeper understanding of what constitutes a particular technique. As well as using Japanese for the names of techniques, we also use it to refer to things such as the place where we train – **dojo**, the instructor – **sensei**, and even the bowing we do – **rei**. In these particular instances, as well as being quite succinct it also forms part of the ceremony involved in training in Jiu Jitsu. These 'ceremonies' have specific purposes. The rei-ing at the beginning and end of a session is a greeting and an agreement to teach/train between instructor and students. The bowing to one another before and after a technique lets partners know when it is safe to begin practice and when they have stopped.

Japanese helps to keep the spirit and clarity of these things in the Jitsuka's mind, none more so perhaps than the use of the word **yamae**. This means stop and is usually the first Japanese word a Jitsuka learns. This word is very important as within the dojo it carries much more than just the word stop. Stop can sometimes be considered a request. All Jiu Jitsuka are taught the weight carried by **yamae** – it's a command and it tends to stand out against the usual English bantering that might take place during a normal training session.

Finally, it's quite fun learning little bits and pieces of Japanese as you progress through your Jiu Jitsu career. It keeps your mind ticking over as you struggle to remember the names of the throws you are doing during the longer sessions, and in a fight it certainly helps to have an alert mind – so perhaps it's good preparation too.

University of York Jitsu Club

will start to move towards applying these techniques in rehearsed and then unrehearsed training situations. At the same time you will be learning many more advanced skills that build on the basic techniques you have already learned. By the time you have started to put all of this together you will have started to practise at a higher level in which focus and intent will be the key component of your training. Everything you do must work. You will be dealing with the unexpected and will have reached a stage at which you are starting to truly master Jiu Jitsu.

## WARMING UP

Warming up before any type of exercise makes a lot of sense. If stress is put on 'cold' muscles or tendons then the chances of injury increases dra-

A typical session may look something like this:

Rei on – formal opening of session

Warm up – 25 mins

Ukemi (falling) and atemi (striking practice) – 20 mins

Syllabus training

Application – 30 mins

Weapons training

Weapons circle training at grade appropriate level and intensity – 25 mins

Ground fighting practice – 10 mins

Warm down – 10 mins

Rei off – formal end of session

matically. This is especially true in Jiu Jitsu where stress and strain is put on almost every part of the body.

The purpose of a warm up isn't to kill you or reduce your chances of completing the training session; warm ups are aimed to prepare you for the session and to help you complete it. At a beginner's level an ideal warm up will last about 25 minutes and should comprise exercises to warm up muscles to their optimum performance level, graduated stretching, repetitions to develop and maintain body strength, exercises to improve reaction time and to develop mental

strength. The best warm ups are both challenging and fun, designed to push you to your limit but not over it. If you are really struggling in a warm up then stop! Improvement only comes over time and there is nothing to be gained from trying to beat a senior grade at sit ups (and hurting yourself in the process) if you have only just started. Your time will come.

Although each instructor will have their own warm up routines, a beginner's warm up session may look something like this:

## Warming up muscles
Running gently on the spot – 2 mins
Gradually pick up pace and bring knees to chest from high jogging position – 2 mins
Star jumps – 1 min
Gentle jogging – 1 min
Squat thrusts – 30 secs

## Developing strength
15 press ups
10 sit ups – left knee bent, hold for 5 secs at upright position
10 sit ups – right knee bent, hold for 5 secs at upright position
Swing both arms in circle forwards and backwards – 1 min
Repeat sequence
10 both knees to chest
Gentle jogging to slow heart rate

# Stretching sequence – repeat three times

**1.** *Stretch up*

**2.** *Touch toes*

**3.** *Press up*

**4.** *Stretch out back*

**5.** *Arch back*

**6.** *Jump through*

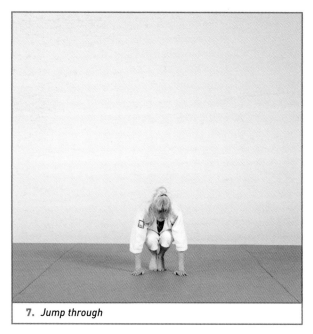

**7.** *Jump through*

**8.** *Jump through*

**9.** *Stretch left*

**10.** *Stretch right*

**11.** *Stretch left*

**12.** *Stretch right*

## Developing strength

Resistance warm up exercises with a training partner can be a lot of fun. Try pushing them and then pulling them as hard as you can while they resist. Do it for 30 seconds each then swap over.

## Developing mental strength

Stretch your arms out in front of you and alternate quickly between clenched fists and open hands for as long as you can – maximum 1 min.

Stretch your arms out to your side and alternate quickly between clenched fists and open hands for as long as you can – maximum 1 min.

Stretch your arms up above your head and alternate quickly between clenched fists and open hands for as long as you can – maximum 1 min.

## Improving reaction time (basic reaction warm up)

You should be as relaxed as possible.

The aim is to touch your partner's hand with the back of your hand.

The only way they can stop you is by moving their hand or body. You are not trying to punch your partner in the face!

Finish off with a group game of tag.

## WARMING DOWN

The warm down at the end of the training session is just as important as the warm up. Following a two hour training session a warm down generally takes about ten minutes and should never be rushed. Focus on gentle stretching. Try to relax all the muscles you have used in the session. Concentrate on your breathing and heart beat – gradually bring them under control. The warm down may end with a period of contemplation – **mokusou**. The aim of mokusou is to try to forget about the world outside and to focus on the Jiu Jitsu session you have just participated in. Don't forget that without you the session would not have been complete.

### TRUE STORY: IT'S GOOD FOR YOUR HEALTH

When I first started Jiu Jitsu I wasn't particularly fit, sporty or flexible. However, after a few weeks of Jitsu I could touch my toes – something I couldn't remember ever being able to do. This was a great personal achievement for me, although my delight was amusing to my girlfriend who had done ballet since a young age and couldn't understand why everyone was not this flexible.

**Richard**

## INJURIES AND ACCIDENTS

Unfortunately injuries are almost unavoidable in Jiu Jitsu and there will be a time when you will pick up an injury. Your instructor will be trained in first aid and will help immediately if you are hurt. You must follow your instructor's advice about injuries, especially if they recommend further medical treatment. There is absolutely nothing to be gained from training with an injury or not allowing sufficient time for an injury to heal before you return to training. You may be really frustrated but think about how much more frustrated you will be if you aggravate your original injury and have to take even more time off.

Jiu Jitsu is a full-contact martial art and the majority of accidents occur either because students do not take sufficient care of their training partner, especially when they are throwing them, or because they are not aware of their distance from other students on the mat. Your instructor will always have overall responsibility for what

### TRAINING TIP

Despite the use of edged and heavy weapons, and painful locks, throws and strikes, serious injuries and bad accidents are very rare in Jiu Jitsu. However, they can occur and it is everybody's responsibility to minimise the chances of them happening by always following the teacher's instructions and training as safely as possible.

happens on the mat but help your instructor as much as possible by making sure that you always have sufficient space in which to train.

## Getting in close

Many martial arts stress the importance of keeping your attacker at arm's length, especially those that focus mainly on kicks and punches. However, the reality is that unless you are very good and really fast and strong at kicking and punching then getting in close and staying close is a much better option. To work effectively, punches and kicks have to be accurate and powerful. Most people can actually take a punch or a kick without being knocked out or knocked down, even though it will hurt. As soon as you are inside the range of the strikes then you are in a much safer position. This is even true on the ground. It may go totally against all your instincts but pulling an attacker down on you and pulling them in close actually reduces their opportunity to hurt you while giving you many opportunities to hurt them. In most cases your attacker will not expect this approach and you will have far more control of the situation than they do.

Some schools of Jiu Jitsu focus almost solely on working on the ground and while this is often devastatingly effective there are a number of factors that can make ground fighting alone questionable. Nowadays more attacks involve weapons, attackers often have friends who are more than happy to get stuck in, especially if you are on the ground. However, ground fighting is incredibly important and in one-to-one situations incredibly effective so quite a lot of space is given to this area from an early stage.

## Thinking about weapons

Training against armed attackers is an integral part of Jiu Jitsu training and as a beginner you will quickly learn about the most common types of attack, how to avoid them and how to defend yourself against them. Training is gradual and, unlike the Samurai, you will be training with imitation weapons for some time before you start to train with the real thing. The weapons you will learn to defend yourself against include wooden coshes, chains, bottles, broken bottles and knives.

### YOI STANCE – THE READY STANCE

The yoi stance is the most basic stance in Jiu Jitsu. Unlike other martial arts Jiu Jitsu is not highly prescriptive about how you stand as ultimately you will need to find a stance that works for you.

You should be sideways on to your uke (training partner) with your legs about shoulder-width apart, knees slightly bent and your arms up in front of you, slightly tucked in, fists clenched. You do not want to be up on your toes, so drop your centre of balance. Mobility and balance is the key to a successful yoi stance.

### BASIC PARRYING AND BLOCKING

Jiu Jitsu uses a combination of parries and blocks to punches, kicks and weapon attacks. Parries

1.

2.

3.

4.

are firm and protective and the intention is to deflect the attack yet still allow the attacker some movement. Blocks are hard and the intention is to stop the attack. To begin with we are going to think about basic parries from single punches. Get used to practising each parry slowly before you speed up.

## MOVEMENT IS ESSENTIAL

Unfortunately most people tend to stay rooted to the spot when they are attacked. In Jiu Jitsu it is often essential to reduce the distance between you and your uke as much as possible rather than try to back away from them. There are some exceptions to this rule but as we have already said, in general the closer you are to your uke the easier it is to deal with them and the more difficult it is for them to attack you. At a basic level get used to closing distance from the outside and inside and combining your movement with parries.

### TRAINING TIP

Introducing movement is also an excellent distracter as it forces your uke – training partner – to try to co-ordinate their own movement rather than just focusing on yours. Simply trying to push one of your uke's arms up and the other down during an attack can be a simple and effective way of changing your uke's focus.

## WEAKENERS

As soon as you are within striking distance you need to be able to attack vulnerable parts of your uke's body quickly and effectively. The purpose of these attacks is to hurt, distract or disorientate your uke rather than render them incapable of continuing the attack, although this is a bonus if it does happen. Unfortunately, in the real world, it is highly unlikely that a single strike will finish off your attacker so a combination of fast strikes is better. The weakeners must be part of a whole technique and they must make sense. It is no use striking an attacker, pushing them backwards and then running after them to throw them over your shoulder the other way.

## KUZUSHI

**Kuzushi** is the term used for breaking an attacker's stability or unbalancing them in some way. In Jiu Jitsu it is really important to break an attacker's balance because firstly it becomes far easier to defend yourself against them and secondly because it can distract the attacker and give you an opportunity to surprise them.

There are three main ways of using *kuzushi* in Jiu Jitsu:

- your direct action (e.g. pulling or pushing as you defend yourself);

- getting your opponent to move in a certain way through a feint or a combination of attacks to vulnerable parts of their body;

- the direct action of your opponent and your counter to their action, as there is almost always a moment in any attack when your opponent is vulnerable because of what they do.

One of the principal mistakes which the novice makes during his first few lessons is the (perhaps not altogether unnatural) trick he has of keeping the arms straight out in front when holding his opponent, in an attempt to 'keep him off'. Since this leads to resistance and consequently flexed muscles, it is a serious fault and one that might even prove dangerous in serious combat, as the arms are far move likely to be broken or dislocated when straightened than when they are bent. Both arms should be limp, and the grip on your opponent's coat a loose one, so that it may be instantly tightened for a throw or quickly released when circumstances require it. Don't resist when your opponent pushes you; rather, increase your pace in that direction and pull him a little at the same time, or vice versa should he pull you.

Don't let him ever get the 'strain' on you, but go with him, if anything a little faster than his pull would cause you to. By following this precept you are almost catching your balance before he makes you lose it, while he is practically losing his and is without the aid of your resistance on which he has been, more or less, depending to help him regain his balance. Thus, in an easy and simple manner, you neutralise his efforts to get you off your balance and at the same time create a favorable opportunity of effecting a throw, by keeping him off his.

Raku Uyenishi

*The Textbook of Ju-Jutsu Ugenishi SK: [sic] as Practised in Japan* (Athletic Publications: London, 1905)

1.

2.

3.

4.

5.

6.

7.

8.

9.

you can only use the **minimum** amount of force to keep yourself safe. Severely injuring your attacker or worse may well result in you getting into a lot of trouble.

*Strike to groin and face*

## FINISHING OFF

Imagine having taken your attacker or attackers to the ground, walking away and then turning to see them getting back up and coming for you again. All your hard work for nothing!

It is crucial that having dealt with your attacker you leave them in a position from which they are not able to continue their attack. This may involve a series of kicks or strikes to vulnerable parts of your attacker's head or body or a combination of joint locks and breaks and strikes. It is obviously crucial in training with your uke that **you do not follow through** when finishing off. In reality it is crucial that you remain in control of yourself at all times. Remember that in the eyes of the law

Psychologically finishing off an opponent is one of the most difficult aspects of Jiu Jitsu as most people do not like the idea of hurting someone else to the point of their being incapacitated. However, Jiu Jitsu is non-compassionate. It is quite simply a question of survival.

## USING KIAI

In Jiu Jitsu, a **kiai** is a short yell given by a Jiu Jitsuka before or during a fight or technique. You

41

will find a kiai incredibly important as it will help you co-ordinate your breathing with your physical activity.

Using kiai can have a number of other benefits, as they can:

■ startle, distract or even demoralise your attacker;

■ help you mentally prepare for fighting as the levels of adrenalin in your body increase;

■ protect your upper body from a strike by providing a rapid escape route for your breath so you don't get winded;

■ protect your lower body by rapidly contracting your stomach muscles to protect your internal organs;

■ provide solid support for atemi strikes;

■ temporarily increase your resistance to pain.

## RIGHT-/LEFT-SIDE TRAINING

Some opponents are right handed, some are left handed; some may attack with both hands and feet at the same time. You will almost certainly have a favourite side but you cannot afford to concentrate on your best side. You must always practise every technique on both sides and you will not have mastered the technique until you can do it equally well on both sides.

## TAPPING OUT

When you practise Jiu Jitsu you do not get extra points for allowing yourself to be hurt. In training you must tap your partner twice – hard – with the flat of your hand to let them know that they have got the technique right or that you are in pain. **If your uke or partner taps you in practise let go immediately**.

## A LITTLE BIT ABOUT ATTACKING

Much of Jiu Jitsu is practised as **embu** – a dual form where one Jiu Jitsuka is the attacker or **uke** (receiver) and the other Jiu Jitsuka is the defender or **tori** (giver). In real life, attackers are committed to their actions. They are trying to land punches or kicks, they are trying to grab you really hard, they are trying to stab you. Obviously in practise there is no intention to hurt but as an attacker you must be totally committed to attack. Strikes must be on target, grabs must be difficult to get out of; you must not let go unless you are convinced your partner has got the technique right. If you do not attack properly then you will be doing your partner a great disservice and will be giving them a false sense of security.

> **TRAINING TIP**
> You must always attack properly! If you don't then you let your partner down and you let yourself down.

# Traditional techniques

## BASIC UKEMI – FALLING

In Jiu Jitsu training it is very common to come across the terms uke and tori. The uke is the Jiu Jitsuka who receives the technique and the tori is the Jiu Jitsuka who gives the technique. In self-defence training this means that you are the tori when you defend yourself and your uke is the attacker. Being able to look after your uke and being able to look after yourself when you are the uke is crucial to your long-term progress in Jiu Jitsu.

Many techniques in Jiu Jitsu involve throwing your uke or attacker from height. Sometimes when you're still standing, you get knocked to the

*This will hurt if you don't know how to land properly*

ground by your uke before you have a chance to defend yourself (that's where ground fighting comes in). If you don't know how to fall properly this can hurt. A lot!

The action of the uke is known as taking **ukemi**, which literally means receiving body; it is the art of knowing how to respond correctly to a throw, push or takedown without getting hurt. That's why the first part of most training sessions is usually devoted to falling patterns – **ukemi kata** to give it its correct name. Done well, **ukemi** may actually save your life and practising can be a lot of fun. **Ukemi** training will help condition your body and mind, and give you the co-ordination and posture you will need to progress in Jiu Jitsu.

An essential component of ukemi is awareness. As an uke you must be able, with experience, to respond quickly to any of your tori's action. By the time you have progressed to green belt you should be able to perform really graceful ukemi and be totally synchronous with your tori.

There are three basic forms of ukemi to learn at yellow belt.

### Ushiro ukemi – backwards fall

Sit on your haunches, arms by your side, tuck your chin into your chest and allow yourself to fall backwards, letting each part of your back contact the ground from the base of your spine to the top of your neck. Try to relax and push the breath out of your lungs as your back meets the ground. Smile.

Now try again with a simple add on. Your arms are in front of you crossed at the wrist. Your hands are cupped. As you roll back your hands and arms meet the mat at the same time as your back. Don't forget, relax, breathe out, and smile.

And one more time with one more, simple add-on. As you fall back, your hands and arms hit the floor at the same time to absorb some of the impact of your roll. You've just done your first back breakfall.

## Yoko ukemi – sideways fall

Get into a half kneeling position; right knee on the ground, left foot on the ground, left leg at a right angle. Draw your left foot past your right knee and fall on to the left side of your body. This is a lot simpler than it sounds. Again relax and breathe out as you hit the floor.

Now use your left hand and arm to absorb some of the impact of the sideways fall.

Repeat the breakfall on the other side; left knee on the ground, right foot on the ground, right hand to absorb the impact of the fall to your right side.

### TRAINING TIP

Breathe out when you are thrown to stop yourself being winded. Always try to make sure that your head and neck are the last parts of your body to hit the floor – they are very vulnerable.

## Mae ukemi – forward breakfall

This can be in the form of a hard slapping breakfall or more of a forward roll-like motion.

1.

2.

There are subtleties in the different types of forward roll but the principle is that when you are pushed forwards you project yourself even further forwards over your shoulder to roll out of danger and to absorb the impact of the fall.

## UKEMI KATA – FALLING PATTERN

Once you have got to grips with the basic principles of breakfalling it is time to move onto a pattern of falling – the ukemi kata. Rolling around the floor may seem like a strange way to start to learn a martial art but learning to fall gives you confidence in physical movement and will improve your co-ordination. The movements you will now learn in the kneeling ukemi kata underpin many of the traditional techniques of Jiu Jitsu where movement is everything. In the photographs they are only shown from one side but you will need to learn them on both sides.

*The starting position*

### Forward roll – left

Imagine your left hand and arm are a third of a wheel rim. Keep your hand and arm fairly firm.

1.

2.

Your head should not touch the floor at all. Use your right hand and arm to breakfall and bring you back up to a kneeling position.

### Forward roll – right

Next time your right hand and arm are the wheel and your left hand and arm break the fall and bring you back up to a kneeling position.

### Backward roll – left

Crouch with your wrists crossed, hands cupped. You are going to roll over your right shoulder. As soon as your back touches the floor you will be using both arms to break the fall. Continue the roll until you have rolled completely over and are back in the position you started from.

3.

1.

47

2.

3.

### Backward roll – right
Next, roll over your left shoulder.

### Sideways roll – left
From a left-hand kneeling position sweep your left knee with your left hand and fall onto the left side of your body. Continue the roll across your shoulders, left to right, until you are back in the position you started from.

1.

2.

3.

### Sideways roll – right

Next time reverse the technique, so you are in a right kneeling position, using right hand and right side of your body. Roll from right to left across your shoulders.

### Standing Ukemi Kata

Once you have gained confidence in the kneeling ukemi kata you will be ready to start the standing form of the kata. You must keep your arms flexed when you roll forwards and reverse the arm, leg, head and shoulder positions when you practise on the other side.

### Standing forwards – left

1.

49

2.

3.

## Standing backwards – left

1.

2.

## Standing side – left

**3.**

**1.**

**4.**

**2.**

## TRUE STORY: UKEMI IN REAL LIFE

One of the areas that we spend a lot of time practising, particularly as lower grades, is ukemi. In the ten years since I started training in Jiu Jitsu this is the only skill that I've used in 'anger'.

As a purple belt I tried to ride down some steps on my bike, which had no rear brake. The result was (quite predictably) that I went over the handlebars. I rolled neatly out of the fall on the gravelly pavement and to my feet. Unfortunately the bike needed carrying home.

The second time was a few years later trying to light a firework. I hesitated too long before running away from the firework. I didn't see the foot-high mesh fence which completely took my feet out from underneath me. This time, though, I got a round of applause for my roll which barely interrupted my continuing run away from the firework.

**Steve**

3.

## KANSETZU WAZA – BASIC JOINT-LOCKING TECHNIQUES

Joint locks can be applied on any part of the body that bends, such as fingers, wrists, elbows, shoulders or knees. In Jiu Jitsu locks are either used as a means to an end, such as getting control of an attacker before you throw them, or as an end in itself when the attacker is thrown using a wrist lock. Sometimes joint locks are used to restrain, control or immobilise an attacker after they have been taken to the ground. In traditional Jiu Jitsu used by the Samurai of feudal Japan locks were also used for interrogation/torture or for immobilising a prisoner before securing him using rope. In modern sports Jiu Jitsu competitions, contests are often ended when one competitor has successfully and completely 'locked up' the other.

> **TRAINING TIP**
>
> It is imperative that you remember the tapping out rule when you practise joint locks. As you will find, it takes comparatively little strength to use any joint lock effectively if you have understood the technique properly.

Don't hurry any of these techniques as they will take time to learn effectively. To begin with they will feel very slow, cumbersome and unrealistic. Don't worry, you've only just started!

### Wrist locks
#### Kote gaeshi – outside wrist twist

As you are attacked with a downward strike, block to the inside, slide your right hand down and immediately take hold of the right wrist in both hands and simultaneously turn the wrist to the outside as you use an elbow strike to your uke's chin to take them down to the ground.

Step through with your inside leg as you continue to apply more pressure on the wrist.

As your uke falls, keep the wrist lock on to control the hand. On the ground continue to increase pressure on the wrist until your uke has tapped out.

*Kote gaeshi on the street*

### Ura kote – reverse twist

Your uke attacks with a thrust to the stomach. Use a cross block – right hand over left for a right-hand attack, left hand over right for a left-hand attack (see photo 1, over).

Kick to your uke's knee and take a firm hold of their arm just above the wrist. Sharply turn your uke's arm and wrist clockwise and at the same time step back sharply with your right foot to apply more pressure at the wrist (see photo 2, over).

As your uke starts to bend, use downward pressure on the wrist to apply the wrist lock. Finish off the technique with a right side kick to your uke's face.

The technique is reversed if you defend yourself against a left-sided attack.

1.

2.

### Koto gatame – inner wrist lock

Your uke grabs hold with both hands and tries to head-butt you. Turn sideways and protect your face by bringing your right elbow into line with your uke's head.

1.

Take your uke's right wrist in both hands, with your fingers on top, and twist it violently 180 degrees clockwise.

If your uke resists the twist, kick across the knee to weaken.

As the wrist reaches the 180-degree turn, push down hard on the wrist with your right hand and simultaneously strike to the inside of your uke's elbow to bend the arm. This will enable you to apply more pressure at the wrist joint.

2.

3.

### *Arm locks*

Practise these slowly to begin with and only speed up once you are confident that you have got the arm lock on properly. To begin with everything will feel very stylised and not at all useful in self-defence. Practise slowly and smoothly. Your uke should not resist as the point is for you to learn the mechanics of the arm locks.

### First arm lock – kujiki gatame – outside arm break

Take a tight grip of your uke's right wrist and make sure their arm is extended and straight.

Holding your uke's arm out from their body, stretch over the top with your left arm and curl back underneath, with your forearm now directly under their elbow. Take hold of your right wrist

1.

2.

1.

2.

with your left hand. Twist your uke's arm anti-clockwise so that their arm starts to bend against the joint.

Now apply downward pressure quickly and forcefully with your right hand.

### Alternative first arm lock – kannuki gatame – inside arm bolt lock

Facing your uke, make sure their right arm is held out from their body. Your left arm curls over and then back under their right arm. This time your left forearm is under the elbow. Your left hand takes a firm grip of your right forearm.

Slightly rotate your uke's right shoulder with your right hand as you lift your left arm quickly, applying pressure under the elbow.

## NAGE WAZA – THROWING TECHNIQUES

Although it will be some time before you are ready to land from these throws at full speed there are many techniques that you can learn to use quickly and effectively. The use of kuzushi – breaking balance – is essential in traditional Jiu Jitsu and is seen in many throws.

Each throw starts from a yoi stance.

### Osotogari – major outer reaping throw

Move inside towards your uke while using an inside block with an open hand to deflect the punch but not stopping your uke's forward movement. Do not attempt to stop the punch completely as your uke will almost certainly have too much weight and momentum behind it.

Drive your right elbow into your uke's mouth or nose to knock him off balance. Remember to pull your strike in training. Keep moving continuously, quickly and smoothly towards the inside of your uke's right arm as you aim to reap their right leg with your right leg.

Reap your uke's leg as hard as you can. You must be totally committed to the throw as your uke must not be able to continue their attack against you. When your uke hits the ground you will have to finish off with a strike to a vulnerable part of their body.

On the street, exactly the same traditional defence can be used against an attacker. In real life most attackers do not know how to

protect themselves when thrown. The hard concrete and kerb will do most of the job for you.

### Kosoto gari – minor outer reaping throw

Move to the outside of your uke's punch while using an outside block with a right open hand to deflect the punch without completely stopping their momentum.

Circle your left hand around your uke's head, grab their chin and pull them back towards you. Your uke must be off balance before you complete the throw. Keep pulling back hard until you feel your uke begin to lose balance. At this point reap your uke's right leg at ankle height with the inside of your left leg.

Once again you must reap your uke's leg as hard as you can at the same time as pulling them backwards (see above). You must be totally committed to the throw, as your uke must not be able to continue their attack against you. The defence is finished off with a strike to a vulnerable part of the body when your uke hits the ground.

On the street the same traditional defence can be used against an attacker with one simple change. Instead of taking hold of your attacker's chin you can either pull back sharply on their hair, take hold of their nose or fish-hook your fingers into the side of their mouth making sure that they cannot bite your hand. Alternately, you can reach over the head and hook your fingers into the space above your attacker's eyes.

## Kosoto gake – minor outer hook

As your uke grabs you under the arms from the front, weaken the grip by simulating a head butt to the face, kneeing the groin and stamping on their toes as quickly as you can. Force your way to your uke's outside.

**TRAINING TIP**

In training make sure you don't complete any of these weakeners as they are potentially very dangerous.

1.

Grab hold of your uke's hair at the base of the hairline with your left hand and cup their head with the palm of your right hand while flicking your fingers towards their eyes. Your aim is to distract your uke by this action; you are *not* trying to blind them by poking them in the eyes.

Sharply rotate your uke's head anti-clockwise and pull towards the floor with your left hand to break their balance.

As your uke's balance is broken, kick into the back of their right knee with the sole of your left foot to take them to the ground.

Follow your uke to the ground, continuing to pull backwards and down as they fall. Finish off with atemi strikes to vulnerable parts of the body.

2.

3.

*Kosoto gake on the street*

## TRUE STORY – MY JOURNEY THROUGH JITSU

I started Jitsu on a whim. I was looking for a school club to join and the benefits of exercise and self-defence skills seemed ideal. I showed up on the first day of club practice ready to do martial art moves or learn how to get out of any attack. What I got was nothing I had expected. Perhaps it was naivety about martial arts on my part that I didn't realise how much physical contact would take place. I never expected to be asked to punch people, apply arm locks or grab someone's face. It was all very new to me to have such personal contact with complete and total strangers. Therein lay Jitsu realisation number one – whether you're making friends or fighting off an unfriendly attack, you can't be afraid to make physical contact.

It didn't take long for me to get over my hesitation towards contact, and in fact I discovered a love of attacking. Having a legitimate reason to punch, throw, kick and roll made a tremendous difference to my stress levels and I soon discovered I was better at the athletic side of the martial art than I ever thought possible. I found I was punching with more force than was ever appropriate for a girl, and my endurance and confidence was increasing the more I learned. Months into regular practice Jitsu realisation number two hit me – everyone is more physically powerful than even they realise; you just have to let go and go for it.

I wasn't aware I was hooked on Jitsu until the sensei asked who wanted gis to be able to train appropriately and eventually grade. The thought of grading excited me tremendously; I knew Jitsu wasn't just a passing fad for me. I had learned too much about myself in such a short time to let it go so easily. After I had my gi, I felt like a real Jitsuka and it was visible in my practice. I found that I became more focused and mindful during sessions. I'm the type of person who is always multi-tasking and thinking ahead, and sometimes have a hard time just being in the here and now. Jitsu helped change that because it requires you to be present and in the moment. Which leads me to Jitsu realisation number three – if you aren't in your body, if you are thinking about something else or if you're distracted in any way, you'll get injured; simple as that. For me, Jitsu was the one thing in my life that truly required me to be present and aware, something I couldn't even do in a meditation practice.

For me Jitsu has been a process of learning about myself and overcoming fears and personal blocks I hadn't really dealt with before. On top of that, I have made fantastic friends I will know for years and years. In the end, what I gained from Jitsu is probably different from what others experience, but has been profoundly meaningful for me. Regardless of the person or their intentions going in, what I can guarantee is that anyone who starts Jitsu practice will get something out of it – and I'm talking about more than just bruises!

Heather

# Self-defence

## ATEMI WAZA – STRIKING TECHNIQUES

### *Targeting vulnerable parts of the body*

The Samurai recognised that it was not possible to protect every part of the body with armour or muscle. Attacking vulnerable parts of the body is simple and effective. In training it is crucial that you recognise the dangers that come with these techniques. They can cause a lot of pain and damage and your training partner is not just your guinea pig. Remember that they will practice the technique on you as well. Do not cause unnecessary pain and always immediately respect the universal sign of submission – the double tap to your uke's arm or back.

At a lower grade Jiu Jitsuka learn to target 24 vulnerable parts of the body. The 24 vulnerable parts are taught within a kata – a pattern of moves – but Jiu Jitsuka will then use them only when necessary and often with another technique. Control is always essential when practising basic atemi as the aim is to learn where they are, not to injure your training partner!

1.

2.

**3.**

**4.**

**5.**

**6.**

7.

8.

9.

10.

**11.**

**12.**

**13.**

**14.**

15.

16.

17.

18.

19.

20.

21.

22.

23.

## ATEMI WAZA AND UNDERARM GRABS

Atemi waza has practical self-defence uses from the earliest stage of your Jiu Jitsu career. Your uke tries to grab you around the body before they head-butt you. Immediately target your uke's mastoids by jabbing both forefingers into the soft spot immediately behind their ears where the jaw meets the neck. Your second fingers should hook into your uke's jaw to prevent them from escaping. Remember to let go as soon as they tap out.

On the street the same technique used effectively can cause excruciating pain, forcing an attacker to let go of you.

24.

*Using atemi waza in self-defence*

## KANSETZU WAZA IN SELF-DEFENCE

From the earliest stages of learning Jiu Jitsu some arm locks can be used in practical self-defence.

### Second arm lock – karada gatame – body lock

Parry a simple right-handed push or single punch while moving to the outside. As your uke's arm moves past your face, slide your right hand down towards their fist – imagine you were sliding your hand down a rope to catch the knot at the end.

Simultaneously step through with your left leg and strike to the face with your left hand. Continuing your forward movement throw your weight onto your uke's right elbow and pull back on the right wrist, locking the arm in a snapping movement.

### TRAINING TIP

In training you must let go of your uke's wrist as you 'snap' on the arm lock to avoid accidentally breaking your partner's arm.

### Alternative second arm lock – katsugi gatame – tall person shoulder carry lock

Parry a simple right-handed push or single punch while moving to the outside. As the uke's arm moves past your face, slide your right hand

1.

2.

down towards their fist – imagine you were sliding your hand down a rope to catch the knot at the end.

Simultaneously step through, half under your uke's right arm, leading with your left leg.

Strike back with your left elbow into the stomach and pull your uke's right arm down onto your right shoulder, locking the arm in a snapping movement.

### Third arm lock – jodan ude garami – upper body arm entanglement

Block a downward right-hand strike with your left arm held at a right angle and your body aligned to support the block.

Immediately bring your right arm up and under your uke's right arm to support your left arm. Your right hand should be over your left hand. Bring your elbows together.

1.

Step through with your right leg, levering your uke's arm backwards as you move past them. Release the lock immediately they tap out.

### Basic parry and block against a plastic bottle

In Jiu Jitsu it is better to learn to walk before you run. This parry and block is effective against real weapons so an empty plastic bottle is a valuable training aid at a lower level. Practise it slowly and smoothly and try not to break the technique into separate parts.

**Straight down:** The uke attempts to strike you straight down on the head. Moving very quickly inside, you parry the bottle attack and strike into the face with an open hand. Trap your uke's arm with the first arm lock – inside arm bolt lock –

2.

kannuki gatame. You need to ensure that the neck of the bottle is under your armpit. As you start to put on the lock simultaneously strike the front of your uke's shoulder joint very hard and quickly with the side of your hand and pull back against the bottle.

**Backhand**: This time your uke tries to hit you with a backhand strike. Move quickly to the outside and block the strike with the outside of both hands, above and below your uke's elbow. The block is very hard and you are throwing your entire weight into the block.

Slide your right hand down your uke's arm to catch the neck of the bottle in your right hand, while simultaneously striking their right elbow with the palm of your left hand. In real life you will be trying to break your attacker's elbow.

## WORKING WITH BASIC GRABS AND STRANGLES

Effective self-defence is generally simple self-defence; techniques that are overcomplicated do not work well in self-defence. Commitment to the techniques is essential as they will only work if you put absolutely everything into them and psychologically prepare yourself to hurt your attacker. Ultimately you are aiming to use each technique as quickly as possible but in training respect your partner, do not follow through on strikes, start slowly and build up speed.

### Hair grabs

This technique will only work against a real attacker if you use it quickly and forcefully.

**Front**: From the front sweep over the arms of your attacker and step back at the same time. Your atemi strike is aimed at your attacker's carotid (one of the two arteries that supply blood to the neck and head).

**Back**: From the back, turn sideways and drop into your attacker. This will help protect your neck. Start by striking the groin and continue by sweeping your arms over the top of your attacker's. As the grab on your hair loosens strike your attacker's carotid.

## Strangles – front

As the hands go around your throat from the front, immediately drop your chin to your chest and step back with one leg.

Your palms need to be touching. Both arms need to push up as quickly and as strongly as you can against your uke's arms, breaking the grip. If the grip does not loosen then you can weaken them by kicking them in the kneecap or stamping on their foot.

The sides of both hands drive down onto your uke's collar bones.

### Strangles – back

From the back, stamp on your uke's toes. Start to turn into your uke, striking their groin as you turn. Push down as hard as you can on your uke's thumb. You are literally trying to break their thumb by forcing it down onto the back of your neck.

Continue turning right under your uke's arm. As you come out from under the arm, strike their elbow hard with the palm of your hand.

## Side of the head from the front

From the front, forcefully strike one of your uke's arms up and the other down. They will find it hard to keep hold as it is difficult to prevent opposing movements. The hand that has pushed up now strikes down to the side of your uke's neck.

## Side of the head from the back

Turn into your uke and try to turn your head to the side to protect your neck and bring their arms closer together. Force one arm in between your uke's arms and strike down hard onto their fore-arms.

Strike to your uke's temple with the same hand you used to break the grip.

## Wrist grabs

Wrist grabs can be very annoying even if they are not the start of a far more serious attack. You will have to use your judgement to decide when a wrist grab is serious or not. In itself, a wrist grab is not a violent action, but if your attacker grabs your wrist intending to immobilise you while they try a more vicious attack then your response must be as to a serious attack. However, to begin with we are going to look at simply breaking out of grabs by going for the space between the fingers and thumb which is always the weakest part of the grip.

*One hand grab – thumb underneath*

> ## TRAINING TIP
> Use your body weight and movement as well as your strength. If the person who has grabbed you is stronger than you and you only try to use strength to break the grip you will almost certainly fail to escape your attacker. When you pull away always keep your hands open, keep your arms rigid and always step back as you try to escape. Your backward step creates momentum and will increase the amount of force you can use in the techniques.

If any of the grabs feel serious then you must use a weakener before you start the wrist releases. The best weakeners against wrist grabs are kicks to the shins and knees as your attacker cannot see what you are doing.

### Both hands on same wrist

With your free hand, reach between your uke's arms and grip your own captured hand; with a jerky motion, push down hard. Your uke will instinctively try to oppose your push by resisting upwards. As soon as you feel your uke's resistance, quickly reverse your action and pull upwards with a jerky movement.

By stepping back at the same time you give yourself even more power to free your wrist.

*One hand grab – thumb on top*

1.

3.

2.

### Both hands on different wrists

Again with a sharp jerky movement push both arms down and outwards. Your uke's normal reaction should be to resist your downward movement. As soon as you feel the resistance with a sharp jerky action, draw your arms inwards and up quickly and sharply. Keep your arms moving until they are in front of your face. Remember to step back.

1.

3.

2.

## HOW LONG WILL IT TAKE?

Training for your yellow belt will generally take three to four months if you train at least twice a week. There is a lot to learn as you take your first steps in Jiu Jitsu so remember to train slowly, only building up speed when you are certain you have fully understood the technique. Don't be afraid to make mistakes – remember this is your first belt in Jiu Jitsu and you are not expected to be an expert just yet.

## TRUE STORY: THROUGH THE PAIN BARRIER

Jiu Jitsu revealed my inner strength. Training the night before my first grading I managed to damage my thumb so badly it swelled to twice its normal size and had to be strapped up. However, I attended the grading and was awarded yellow with two orange! Then I allowed myself to be carted off to A&E! It was most definitely one of my proudest achievements to date.

Natalie

# CHAPTER **THREE** orange belt

The orange belt is the second stage of your journey in Jiu Jitsu. By the time you have gained your orange belt you will know how to apply the techniques you learned for your yellow belt and have started to acquire a range of new techniques. You will be able to pick up new techniques quickly and will be able to practise them in more realistic situations. Most importantly, you will be applying techniques effectively and in some cases without too much thinking.

## PROGRESSION TECHNIQUES

At orange belt level you will also start to see progression techniques that build upon skills you have already learned. By the time you reach black belt almost every aspect of Jiu Jitsu will be a progression where everything you do intuitively fits together with something else.

## Traditional techniques

MORE UKEMI

At orange belt level more emphasis is put on falling properly. You will be learning new throws and as an uke you will be thrown far quicker and from a greater height. It makes sense to know how to protect yourself against possible injuries that result from falling.

Although Jiu Jitsu is practised in the dojo on tatami – rubber or occasionally straw mats – it is used practically in situations where the ground is often hard and uneven. In real life it is very likely that your attacker may get the better of you before you are able to get the upper hand. Being pushed, punched or thrown to the ground can cause a lot of damage so you will need to minimise the chances of injury as much as possible.

## SPREADING THE LOAD

It's essential to spread the load as much as possible when you fall so try to make sure you spread your body weight evenly when you fall. Keep your body as flat as possible to spread the load, keep the sharp parts of your body tucked in and remember that you are not a sack of potatoes.

Don't forget to breathe out as you hit the mat.

## Backwards

Sit on the back of your partner and allow yourself to slide down their side onto the tatami. Keep your head in as you hit the mat, breathe out and remember to breakfall with both arms. As you develop confidence, continue the backward breakfall by rolling over a shoulder and back up into a yoi stance.

## Drop

The drop will protect your face and body against injury if you are pushed or thrown onto your front.

From a crouching position allow yourself to fall forwards. Keep your feet in contact with the mat at all times. Keep your knees flexed and bent. Your hands should be open, palms cupped. As

you hit the mat check your points of contact – the insides of your feet and each arm, from your elbow to your hand, should be in contact with the mat. Your head should be turned to the side to avoid head-butting the floor.

Then, from a standing position with your feet together, let yourself fall forwards into the drop. As you become more comfortable with the drop start jumping in the air before you drop.

Learning to fall from height onto your side, either from a throw in training or from a push or punch in a real attack, is essential if you are to protect yourself against serious injury. If you are confident enough to throw yourself around then you will soon develop the confidence you need to be able to train hard with everyone else in your club. Both of the next two techniques will really help your ukemi skills but, like everything else you do in Jiu Jitsu at this stage, start slowly and don't build up speed or height until you are happy with what you can already do.

Take hold of your uke's belt with your right hand and flip yourself over, leading with your right shoulder as if you were going to do a forwards breakfall, landing on your left side.

Holding your uke's gi with your left hand jump up and double kick their left arm and fall landing on your right side, taking care to spread the load when you land.

*Over the belt*

*Side drop/kick up and drop*

## KANSTEZU WAZA

### Arm locks

At orange belt level you need to start practising arm locks at speed. They are no longer just techniques; they are starting to become defences as well. New arm locks should be practised slowly and only speed up once you are confident that you have got the arm lock on properly. You will be surprised how quickly you will pick them up. Remember to keep looking after your uke.

### Sixth arm lock – ude gatame – straight arm lock

The emphasis at this level is to learn to keep your uke moving throughout the technique. From a right-arm straight punch, step to the outside of your uke's arm. Parry the strike between the wrist and elbow and slide your right hand down towards your uke's wrist.

Take hold at the wrist and rotate it clockwise while still pulling your uke forward. As the wrist turns, strike the point of your uke's elbow and,

### TRUE STORY: A BAD DAY AT THE OFFICE

When I came to London to study I lived in Camden Town. Worried about the strange faces wandering around at night and as I wanted to try a sport I'd never done before, I thought a martial art might be best for me. I'd heard that even small girls like me can defend themselves effectively against the big guys, so I went to my first Jiu Jitsu training and was very impressed by the few simple techniques I was taught during that first two-hour session.

About two months after I had started training at the dojo, I had a really bad day; after that evening's Jiu Jitsu training session I just wanted to go home. Settling myself on a crowded bus, there were two very drunken men close to me, arguing with people on the bus, scaring little girls (which made me particularly angry) and shouting loudly. After refusing to quieten down and curb their language things turned nasty and it seemed as though a fight was going to start. At that point I couldn't take any more and I went in between the two to stop it all. The 'bad' guy was surprised at first but then went for me. I didn't really think about it but basically I shot my index finger at the point just above his collarbone – just as I had been taught by my sensei in case of an emergency. The technique worked; the drunken man stumbled backwards and I had enough time to run to the bus driver, get him to stop the bus and make him call the police. Then I ran all the way home.

What really makes me proud of this experience is that as soon as I was home and calmed down, I realised how dangerous the situation had been for me and that I had done something pretty silly. I am sure I wouldn't have thought that if my sensei had not always explained to us that we should always avoid violence whenever possible. So now I am pretty convinced Jitsu is a superb defensive sport as it doesn't only teach how to get out of trouble, but to stay out of trouble too.

**Anne**

keeping pressure on the elbow, pull forwards and drive them towards the ground.

## ATEMI WAZA

### Blocking to the inside and outside

Hard blocking is actually one of the least effective ways of stopping an attack. In reality it is very dif-

ficult for an extremely small person to effectively block a much stronger, heavier or taller attacker. However, in some situations there is no alternative to blocking an attack and some techniques work best when they are combined with hard blocks rather than softer parries. Blocks must always be combined with strong and stable body movements as you are using your direct force against your attacker's direct force.

Always protect your head and keep your elbows in to protect your body. The blocks are delivered with a whipping and snapping action and a follow-up atemi strike. The side of your open hand is the first point of contact with your attacker and in real life situations you are trying to break bones with the block. When you train you are trying to develop quick reactions but begin slowly. Make obvious movements when you attack so that your partner can first learn the proper techniques of blocking. As you improve, ask your partner to punch quicker and harder. When you feel comfortable with the blocking techniques ask your partner to vary the speed, power and predictability of the strikes.

## TRAINING TIP

Your arms will get sore when you practise any kind of blocking. This is quite normal but don't carry on practising if your arms become painful. You are meant to be enjoying your training.

*Outside block with two hands from back-hand attack, palm to face*

*Inside block with two hands from roundhouse, fist to face*

*Cross block to strike to stomach/groin, back fist to face*

*Block to side of body from strike to kidneys, palm to face*

## NAGE WAZA – THROWING TECHNIQUES

Many throwing techniques in Jiu Jitsu evolved from techniques discovered by other cultures that were assimilated over a period of time into some Japanese martial arts. They became popular in feudal Japan because they were useful in unarmed combat against Samurai in armour. If one were disarmed in the course of combat, throwing techniques were the Samurai's last line of defence as they could be used to bring an armed or unarmed opponent to the floor. Throws were used against a variety of attacks ranging from kicks and punches to katana. The Samurai generally tried to avoid following their attacker to the floor, preferring to finish them off with what-

ever weapon was at their disposal but occasionally the throws moved into a ground-fighting stage. As throwing techniques developed they began to be grouped into throwing techniques with similar characteristics – some throws used leg sweeps, others used hip movements and shoulder pins, some were linear while others were circular in movement.

In each of these throws you must have a tight grip of your uke and you must be beneath their centre of balance before you start to throw. Let your uke fall forwards onto you and only start to lift them when you feel they have lost their balance. Make sure your knees are bent and that your feet are to the inside of your uke's feet.

The entry to each throw at orange belt is similar as you move inside of the punch, leading with your right leg and parrying the punch with your left arm.

**TRAINING TIP**

Remember to use kuzushi in each of these techniques. Your uke must be moving before you throw, so parry the punches, don't block them and stop the momentum of your uke. Practise this on the right and left side, start slowly and build up speed.

91

## O goshi – major hip throw

Gather the moving arm into your body and slide your right arm under your uke's left armpit.

Pivot on your right foot until your hips are parallel with your uke's hips, pulling them tightly into you as you turn.

**TRAINING TIP**

Throwing techniques should be as effortless as possible. If you are putting a huge amount of physical effort into the throw then you are doing it wrong. It is really important not to slow the momentum of the attack. To begin with practise each throw slowly and smoothly and don't speed up until you are comfortable with the throw.

In training learn to use each throw against right and left arm punches. You will have to use your common sense and ask for your instructor's help as each throw in this book is only shown against a right-side punch.

Drop under your uke to break their balance and continue to lift with your right arm and pull around with your left, using your uke's movement to allow you to lift and draw them over your hips.

Pivot on your right foot until your hips are parallel with your uke's hips, pulling them even more tightly into you as you turn.

Simultaneously strike to the face and groin to finish off.

### Ippon seoi nage – one-arm shoulder throw

Gather the right hand punch tightly into your body and slide your right arm under your uke's right armpit. Lift them at the armpit.

93

Drop under your uke to break their balance and continue to lift with your right arm and pull around with your left, using your uke's movement to allow you to lift and draw them over your hips to complete the throw.

Simultaneously strike to the face and groin to finish off.

1.

Pivot on your right foot until your hips are parallel with your uke's hips. Your right foot then extends to cover your uke's right foot. Keep pulling your uke even more tightly into you as you turn.

### Seoi otoshi – shoulder drop
Gather the right-hand punch tightly into your body and slide your right arm under your uke's right armpit. Lift your uke at the armpit.

2.

Drop under your uke to break their balance and continue to lift and pull around with your right arm. Pull around with your left, using your uke's movement to allow you to lift and draw them over your right leg to complete the throw.

1.

Pivot on your right foot until your hips are parallel with your uke's hips, pulling them tightly into you as you turn.

Drop under your uke to break their balance and continue to pull around with your left arm, using your uke's movement to complete the throw.

Lock the arm as your uke hits the ground. Simultaneously strike to the face and groin to finish off.

3.

Simultaneously strike to the face and groin to finish off.

### Koshi guruma – hip wheel
Gather the moving arm into your body and slide your right arm around your uke's neck.

95

2.

3.

### Finishing off

In each of these throws drop to a squatting position over your uke at the end of the throw. Pin their arms and then simultaneously strike to the throat and groin.

## TRUE STORY: THOSE WHO CAN . . .

I started Jitsu purely because I wanted to try something different. To be honest, I kept going in those first few weeks, despite the bruises and the aches and pains, because I met some great people at the club and training really was something we all did on the way to the social afterwards.

However, without Jitsu I would never have gained the confidence I now have in myself and my convictions that enabled me to become a teacher. I had always thought about the possibility of a career in teaching but never believed it was a real option for me because I was too shy and quiet to even stand up in front of 30 noisy children, let alone keep control of them! But ask any of my training partners now and they'll assure you that if there's one thing I'm not these days it's quiet and retiring!

Jitsu has taught me some amazing things. As a small girl, I never thought I'd be able to defend myself against armed attackers twice my size, let alone make it look vaguely impressive in a martial arts kind of way. I can now do both to a level that far surpasses my initial expectations. However, most of all, Jitsu has taught me things about myself I don't think anything else could. I now know that with a bit of self-belief I can rise to any challenge and achieve far more than I would ever have thought possible. My career and current class of 30 very active seven-year-olds are testament to that!

Jo

## OSAEKOMI WAZA – GROUNDWORK TECHNIQUES

### *Starting groundwork*

Many martial artists and self-defence instructors tell their students never to go to the ground with an attacker because of the dangers to be found there. This is almost always true of martial arts that focus mainly on punching and kicking. Fighting on the ground is seen as dirty, unskilled, uncontrolled and uncontrollable.

In some ways it does make sense to avoid going to the ground if you can – after all, who really wants to get tangled up with an attacker and roll around in the gutter if you don't need to. Fighting from the ground doesn't make much sense either if there is more than one attacker, although sometimes you can use an attacker as a shield against the others or if your attacker has a weapon.

However, statistics show that over half of real-life confrontations eventually end up on the ground anyway, so it makes sense to know what to do. Occasionally, fighting from the ground is the safest place to be, especially if your attacker is someone who knows how to kick and punch, given that there are so many different ways that they can strike or move from a standing position. At other times you may be in control of an attack but then find that the tables are completely turned when your attacker lands a lucky punch or kick. In some schools of Jiu Jitsu the Jiu Jitsuka's goal is to almost always take the fight to the ground as quickly as possible, as on the ground everything slows down and it is far more difficult

97

for the attacker to generate much force to their strikes the closer they are to you.

Getting your attacker to the floor normally happens in one of two ways, through a throw or through a takedown. Very occasionally you may be lucky enough to knock an attacker to the floor, but this is very unlikely.

> **TRAINING TIP**
> There is no need to go to the ground with an attacker after you have thrown them if it looks like your attacker won't be getting back off the ground in any great hurry.

The important distinction between throws and takedowns is that a throw uses minimum physical strength, maximum use of kuzushi and optimum movement, while a straightforward unrefined takedown often uses a lot of physical strength, and there is very little art to the method of breaking balance.

Although takedowns can be effective if you are big and strong, they are generally very difficult for a smaller person to execute on a bigger person – the smaller person simply doesn't have the physical strength or body weight to drag or knock the bigger person to the floor. To force an attacker to the floor without the use of kuzushi means brute force over skill or technique. If you are able to use kuzushi then it is far more likely to have been by accident rather than skilled

manipulation of your attacker's movement and balance.

*This is a very vulnerable position*

Because Jiu Jitsu was developed for real life situations where you have to control an attacker while defending yourself, learning to fight on the ground will become a vital part of your armoury. Groundwork techniques put you in a position where your attacker cannot strike you, but you could, if you chose to, strike them and as the techniques are based on skill and application they allow a smaller person to wear out a larger and more aggressive one. Groundwork techniques focus on hold downs, joint locks and carotid restraints (more about this later). Although some techniques focus on pressure points and targeting vulnerable parts of the body,

*Pulling your attacker onto you is far safer*

**TRAINING TIP**

Most ground fighting techniques focus on hold downs, joint locks and carotid restraints. This means that the Jiu Jitsuka does not have to be stronger than their attacker, they only have to be stronger than the attacker's weakest point – usually their elbow, shoulder, ankle or neck – or have a lower centre of gravity if their attacker tries to turn them over.

most do not as at a lower level of Jiu Jitsu many Jiu Jitsuka are not, mentally conditioned to strike vulnerable areas. Most ground fighting goes against an attacker's natural instincts. If they go to the ground they want to create space between them and their victim so they can follow up the attack with more strikes. It is therefore a lot safer for the defender to pull the attacker in to them to reduce the chances of the strikes actually landing or having any power behind them.

At orange belt, groundwork techniques are relatively easy to understand and you will pick them up quickly. You will soon learn that your uke's reactions to your movements will be very predictable. The more skilled you become the easier it will be to move your uke around.

As with all other techniques start slowly and build up speed. However, groundwork does give you the opportunity to be very physical in training and acquire some of the physical hardening you will need as you progress. Once you have understood the techniques, practise them hard and ask your uke to really struggle to try to get out of them.

**TRAINING TIP**

To avoid injury, start by practising these techniques from the ground. You will start to use them in conjunction with throws and more refined takedowns once you are confident that you can land properly from throws.

### Starting point

Face your uke and take hold using a traditional grip. Left hand to upper right of gi. Right hand to left sleeve at elbow. Your uke makes the same movements.

### Keza gatame – scarf hold

With your left hand leading turn into your uke, pulling backwards with your right hand as you turn. Your uke will fall onto their back. Continue the turn, tightening your grip on your uke. Pull their right arm tightly into you, spread your legs wide and keep your head low to the ground to lower your centre of gravity as much as possible. Ask your uke to try to free themselves. Keep practising until you can keep the hold on for at least 30 seconds.

### Kata gatame – shoulder hold

Allow your uke to free their left arm. As they start to pull it out push their arm across their face, swap your legs over and drive your left shoulder and head into your uke's arm, squeezing as tightly as you can. You are aiming to use a hold down and a carotid restraint. **This technique can be very dangerous; you must let go if your uke taps.** Again ask your partner to struggle and to hit you. Try to keep the hold on for 30 seconds or until your uke taps.

## TRUE STORY: A JOURNEY THROUGH JIU JITSU

I started Jiu Jitsu in July 2006 because I wanted to try something new. I wanted to develop some new skills and to challenge myself.

Firstly, I was very bad at it. I couldn't memorise any of the syllabus as I didn't feel confident enough to repeat it when all the novices were looking at me. I tried to catch up by doing some falls in the gym but it took me many weeks to understand how to move, how to fall and how to kick the pad. I felt that I had to prove to myself that I could do it. I simply couldn't give it up. After five months of Jiu Jitsu I got my yellow belt. I felt happy because I knew that I had had to fight my fears and I gained much confidence achieving it.

Secondly, I decided not to stop my sessions because for two or three hours a week, I was becoming a pupil and I had to listen carefully to my teachers. Sometimes, I was very tired or I'd just had a bad day and I simply couldn't concentrate. But this reminded me that in the classroom, you have to be able to understand circumstances and different needs, and that if my teacher gave up on me I would never learn. This helped me when I went back to my teaching job the following morning: I remembered my struggles and how patient my sensei were. It was like a perfect reminder about how to teach, so everyone could achieve their best – even if it takes a long time.

Thirdly, for me, Jiu Jitsu is not only about self-confidence, self-discipline and life skills, it is also about being fit and meeting new people.

Today, I still struggle with many techniques but I've understood that Jiu Jitsu gives me the chance to explore the unknown and recap what I've known from a different perspective.

**Witold**

### Yoko shiho gatame – side four-quarters hold

Let your uke free their left arm again and gather it under your body. Drop your chest between your uke's stomach and chest. Your left arm goes in between your uke's legs and grips the leg nearest you. Your right arm goes over and under your uke's left shoulder. Ask your uke to shift their balance and experiment (with your legs in with knees touching your uke's body) or out. Feel how your leg position affects your uke's ability to get out. Again ask your uke to try to escape or land effective strikes to your body. You will be hit but find a good position to minimise your uke's movement.

Now try everything on the other side!

Yoko shiho gatame

# Self-defence

## ATEMI WAZA

### Kicks, strikes and punches

In Jiu Jitsu atemi is often used in conjunction with locks and throws. Kicks are almost always kept below waist level and target the groin, knees, shins and ankles. Strikes and punches are always aimed at vulnerable parts of the body like the eyes, temples or carotid.

### Basic mawashi geri – roundhouse kick

As your uke punches, simultaneously block the punch, lift your kicking leg, swivel from your hips and use mawashi geri with the top part of your foot to the inside of your uke's knee.

Although in a real situation you are aiming to break your attacker's knee, in training you must ensure that you do not follow through with the kick or use maximum force. Your uke can protect themself during training by falling sideways away from the direction of the kick.

### Yoko geri – side kick

This is one of the most powerful of all the kicks used in Jiu Jitsu, especially when aimed at the ribs or solar plexus. You can strike by using either the side or the heel of the foot. When training use the side of your foot when striking at the throat or neck if your uke has been brought down, whereas the heel of the foot is best for all other targets such as the solar plexus, ribs or kidneys.

As your uke lunges towards you, drop your weight on to your back foot, keeping both arms up to protect your face and to absorb some of the impact of the punch.

Start the kick by bringing your knee up and then twisting sideways, thrusting your leg forwards at your uke while rotating your body on the supporting leg. You can bend your supporting leg while kicking to give yourself better balance. Your target is the floating rib or the side of your uke's knee.

Your foot is pointed sideways with your toes pulled tightly upwards and the striking surface is the side of the foot or the heel.

**TRAINING TIP**
Whenever you use kicks to defend yourself you must return your leg to the ground quickly to stop your uke from grabbing your leg.

## Mae geri – front kick

Mae geri is the most used of all kicks in martial arts in general, because it can be performed very fast with little wind-up, and it is very difficult to block if the uke keeps their distance. However, mae geri is not that useful in close contact defences as there is normally not enough space to generate the momentum needed for the kick to work effectively. There are slight variations in how

103

to perform a front kick, from a quick snap kick to a very powerful thrusting front kick.

Your uke punches to your stomach. Use a double block to stop some of the impact of the punch and move into the second wrist lock you have already learned at yellow belt – ura kote.

It's crucial that you return your leg to the ground quickly to stop it from being grabbed if the kick does not work. If the kick does not work effectively, there is nothing apart from the uke's own movements to stop you kicking again.

As your uke's head starts to drop, start your kick by bringing your knee up and forwards. The heel and then the toes must spring forwards from the ground in one movement, snapping the leg forwards towards your target. Your target is your uke's face, which has been dragged down to below hip height. As you kick you can bend your supporting foot to give better balance. The striking surface is the top of your foot. Thrust your hips forwards with the kick to add power and speed.

### Hiza geri – using your knees

In Jiu Jitsu you are always trying to close down distance between you and your opponent and strikes with your knees are often more effective than kicks.

Hiza geri and maewashi hiza geri – roundhouse knee kick – are very powerful close-quarter techniques mainly used to the groin, stomach or head. Maewashi hiza geri can also be done from the side to attack the ribs.

## TRAINING TIP

Grabbing your uke and pulling them into your knee kick makes the knee strike even more powerful.

Move to the outside of your uke and parry the punch across your body. Using your rear leg, push off powerfully from your toes and force your knee into your uke's stomach or groin.

If your uke is heavier, you can simultaneously jump and pull yourself, knee first, into the defence.

To complete the technique and take your uke down to the ground you can either grab their hair

and yank them down to the ground or use kostogari and take them down to the ground where you must finish them off.

Against heavier opponents, pull yourself into them, knee first. Opponents of similar or lesser weight can be pulled into the knee to make the technique more effective.

### Strikes with the hand

In Jiu Jitsu strikes are normally used as a means to an end, rather than an end in themselves. However, it is still important to make the strikes as effective as possible. Striking hard takes total commitment and focus. In training you are pulling strikes as you do not want to hurt your uke. In real life each strike is intended to damage your attacker.

## Open hand

As your uke punches to your head with their right fist, step to the inside and block with your left open hand, keeping your right hand in front of your face. After you have blocked, drop your left arm over your uke's right arm and, pulling them towards you, drive the heel of your right-hand palm into your uke's nose. Your fingers should be directly over your uke's eyes.

Keep moving as you use the strike. As your uke rocks backwards, continue stepping through into osotogari – major outer reaping throw.

This time, block across your body with a right open hand block as your uke punches you. After you have blocked, grab their wrist and immediately pull them towards you as you counter their attack by driving the left palm heel to their face.

Some points to remember:

- if you block right arm to right arm and pull your opponent's arm downwards, it becomes far more difficult for them to launch another attack against you;

- do not try to catch your opponent's arm. You must block first and then grab their arm;

- make sure you get a good grip by getting your thumb and fingers tightly around their wrist. If you grab too far up their forearm you will not

1.

2.

get a good grip. Slide your hand down to the wrist where their arm is not so large and you can get a better grip;

- if the attack is fast and powerful, step to the side and buy yourself some time. Try something different.

### Using your fist

Blocking across your body and striking back with the same arm is an effective way of protecting your face at the same time as countering an attack. You need to have closed hands in your yoi stance. From a right punch to the upper body move your right forearm from the side and across your chest, holding your forearm near vertical, bent at the elbow at an angle of about 90 degrees

in relation to your upper arm. Lead this movement with your elbow. Simultaneously, your other arm returns to the ready position, tucked under your left shoulder. Upon impact with your uke's forearm, complete the blocking movement by twisting your right forearm, causing the attack to roll off your arm.

Immediately after completing the block, counter attack with an uraken uchi – back fist strike – to your uke's temple.

It's very important to lead the strike from your elbow and to snap your wrist to gain extra speed and power in your strike.

Now practise the block and strike on the left side.

## Simultaneous strikes

Striking two vulnerable parts of the body at the same time can be a very effective way of weakening an attacker. At a lower grade, moving to the outside of an attacker is generally safer than moving inside as you have a better chance of getting away if you forget what to do.

Practise this block and strike slowly to get used to simultaneous movements. As your uke lunges at you with both hands, step to the outside and block across your body with your left arm to your uke's right arm.

Drive your right arm into your uke's groin at the same time as aiming a back fist strike to their head.

## KANSETSU WAZA

As your uke's punches parry to the inside, strike to the face with the heel of your hand. Apply kannuki gatame – inside arm bolt lock – to your uke's arm.

As you apply the arm lock, break your uke's balance by pushing up and back on the arm.

Facing your uke, make sure their right arm is held out from their body. Your left arm curls over and then back under their right arm. This time your left forearm is under the elbow. Your left hand takes a firm grip of your right forearm.

Slightly rotate your uke's right shoulder with your right hand as you lift your left arm quickly, applying pressure under the elbow.

### *Fourth arm lock – gedan ude garami – lower-level arm entanglement*

The arm entanglement is one of the most effective locks in Jiu Jitsu but it requires considerable practice to get it to work properly. Start slowly and only build up speed when you are confident you understand the technique properly.

It is essential to use an effective and hard block as your uke aims a roundhouse strike to your kidneys. Use a whipping movement to block with an open hand just above the wrist.

Your uke's arm should be blocked at least 12 inches from your body.

Cut in hard with your right hand at the elbow and keep applying a lot of pressure at the wrist. Keep pushing the arm until it is behind the back.

The uke's arm needs to be horizontal. Lift your uke from the chin as you trap their elbow in your stomach to increase leverage at the elbow and shoulder.

### Fifth arm lock – hiji gatame – elbow lock

Again it is essential to use a hard block to stop your uke as they aim to strike your stomach or groin. Use a whipping movement to your uke's wrist as you use a cross block to stop the attack at least 12 inches from your body.

## TRAINING TIP

Remember to always block with your hands as fists when you use a cross block. Your legs should be well apart with considerable force applied to the wrist.

As soon as you have stopped your uke's movement take hold of their wrist with your top hand and start to rotate their arm clockwise.

## TRUE STORY: A DANGEROUS MIX

I once sat in as an observer on a mixed grading where martial artists from a range of different martial arts had decided to try to combine elements of their particular art into a general grading. I was very much against this and thought it was a little like trying to combine golf with baseball. As the martial artists tried out their particular skills one of the grading panel produced a set of very sharp double-sided knives for the black belts.

Alarm bells started to ring in my head as I knew that some of the black belts would never have trained against real knives. Two of the black belts who trained in Jiu Jitsu showed their skills against the knives and were quite good. The next black belt got up and I realised straight away that he was more practised in kicking and punching. With a sinking feeling I watched him 'dance' around the opponents, blocking as if he was fencing. He blocked a knife attack to the groin with his open hand and, as I watched, a ring of blood developed around his little finger and I realised he had almost severed his little finger from his hand.

**Brian**

As their arm reaches the highest point, push down sharply on the elbow.

Draw out their arm and keep pressure on the elbow. Use chest pressure to keep the arm lock on.

## NAGE WAZA – USING THROWS IN SELF-DEFENCE

### o uchi gari – major inner reap from kick

As your uke aims a straight kick to your groin, parry the kick as you step to the inside of the attack. Drive your hand into your uke's face, knocking their head backwards.

Catch the kicking leg and step through to sweep away the other leg.

As your uke hits the ground, step in to strike their groin.

**TRAINING TIP**

Practise the defences slowly against gentle grabs but start doing them quickly against hard attacks as soon as you feel you are making progress. The emphasis here is on effectiveness. Don't worry if the technique feels messy – first and foremost it has to work. Remember to pull your strikes when you practice.

### Overarm grab front

Drive your hand into your uke's groin and simultaneously head-butt them.

As you feel the uke's grip loosen, turn into them, drop under your uke's point of balance and turn into o goshi.

**TRAINING TIP**

Many Jiu Jitsuka find that falling from o uchi gari can be painful and it is vitally important to look after your uke, especially if they are not confident about falling backwards. Help your uke by supporting them in the small of the back as they fall backwards. Don't stop supporting them until they are confident that they can handle the fall.

### Defence against body grabs

A combination of strikes to vulnerable parts of the body, throws and locks are very effective against body grabs.

As you take your uke's weight, drive up with your right arm and pull around with your left. Strike to their face and groin as your uke hits the floor.

you pull down sharply on your uke's head to take them to the floor.

And finish off.

1.

### Underarm grab front

Drive your forefingers and thumbs into your uke's mastoids (the bony lumps behind the ears) – the fourth strike to vulnerable parts of the head – to loosen their grip. You can also drive your knee onto your uke's groin, scrape your foot down their shin (fifth strike to the body) and stamp on their toes (sixth strike to the body).

Twist their head using their chin and hair or ear and as your uke starts to turn, bring the inside of your left foot into the back of your uke's right knee.

Stamp into the back of their knee as you continue to turn their head, applying kosoto gake as

2.

3.

1.

### Overarm grab from behind

Strike into your uke's nose with the back of your head and stamp on their toes.

As their grip loosens, throw both arms forwards; drop your weight, take hold of one of your uke's arms and bring them around the front of the body using seio otoshi.

Finish off with a kick to the small of the back.

2.

## Underarm grab from rear

As you strike into your uke's nose with the back of your head, stamp on their toes. Strike the back of their hand between the base of the fingers and wrist as hard as you can with your knuckles. The strike is delivered in a downward movement.

Push sharply on one of your uke's hands to apply the second wrist lock – ura kote.

Step around your uke, keeping tight hold of the wrist. Keep moving until you have straightened their arm. You must keep pressure at the wrist throughout the movement.

Finish off by kicking to their head.

2.

1.

3.

# Introducing weapons defences

Being threatened or attacked by someone holding a weapon can be incredibly scary and there have been many discussions and arguments in martial arts about the stage at which students should begin to learn defences against weapons. Indeed some martial arts do not teach them at all, while others only teach them at a very senior level. To complicate matters further, even when weapons defences are taught some martial arts focus on the best offence being a very good defence, while others concentrate on the best defence being a very good offence. Martial arts students can be left feeling very confused by the whole philosophy of dealing with weapon attacks; is it best to imagine that an attacker's knife makes no difference to the attack, and to simply defend as usual? Perhaps it is better to adapt the technique defensively to avoid the possibility of being slashed or stabbed? Or is it better to learn a new series of defences specifically designed against weapons attacks? This can be taken to another level when students start to think about the techniques they can use to get away from weapon-wielding attackers and techniques they can use to control and deal with armed attackers. And always at the back of the mind is the thought that if the attacker is using the weapon 'functionally' to get something off you, like your wallet, then maybe it is just common sense to give the attacker what they want anyway.

Obviously, in our modern world some weapons defence are less effective because of the ways in which the weapons have been designed to be used. Firearms can be used from a distance so gun defences are only feasible when the attacker is close enough for you to be able to grab the hand holding the gun or move yourself to a position in which it is difficult for the attacker to actually point the gun at you.

Jiu Jitsu has a common sense approach to weapon attacks. As in all aggressive situations, a defensive approach is usually considerably safer than an offensive one. If you are threatened with a weapon, escape or defusing the situation in any way is always preferable to an aggressive response, which may lead to severe injury or even death. Unlike punches, kicks or grabs, a single blow to the back of the head with a heavy cosh or metal bar can kill, one thrust of a knife can kill, a single bullet can kill. Avoidance is always the best strategy.

Unfortunately, nowadays we seem to live in a society where violence is more common. Much of this violence involves weapons of some kind and much of the violence appears to be based on the attacker's aim of simply hurting the victim as

## TRAINING TIP

In Jiu Jitsu, weapons defences are taught from an early stage, with the main emphasis being on getting in as close as possible to the attacker. It is very difficult for any attacker to use a weapon effectively if you are so close to them that they are unable to use it accurately.

much as possible. Defusing situations or running away is simply not always an option, and the need to try defend yourself has become a priority.

To begin with, practise these weapons defences slowly. If you are not ready for the attack ask your uke to stop. It is crucial that you do not attempt to block the weapons themselves – you will break your arms. Your main aim is to get inside the circle of the attacks.

> **TRAINING TIP**
>
> If you are worried about practising against real weapons then start by practising the techniques with empty plastic bottles. When you progress to 'real' coshes start by using wooden batons about 25 centimetres long.

### Koshi guruma – roundhouse cosh attack

Move to the inside of the attack, within the arc of the cosh. The attacking arm is parried. Do not block. It is important not to slow the momentum of the attack.

Gather the moving arm into your body and slide your right arm around the uke's neck and into koshi guruma, using your uke's movement to complete the throw.

Lock the arm before you remove the cosh, simultaneously striking to the face and groin to finish off.

### Kosoto gake – backhand cosh

Move to the outside of the attack and block the attacking arm with the side of both hands.

As the uke is pulled backwards and off balance, stamp at the back of their knee using kosoto gake.

Disarm using an arm bolt or lock and simultaneously strike to the face and groin to finish

Immediately grab hold of the back of the uke's hair and pull back sharply towards the ground.

119

## TRUE STORY: A LUCKY ESCAPE?

I was an orange belt, so had only been doing Jitsu for probably no more than six months. Travelling home from a training session one evening I sat on the top deck of the bus along with a dozen or so teenagers.

No sooner had I settled into my seat, listening to my Walkman near the stairwell, when one of the group came down and ripped the headphones out of my ears, snatched the Walkman out of my hands and took it to the back of the bus. I didn't do or say anything. Soon I was surrounded by other members of the gang, one of whom claimed he had a knife and was going to use it unless I gave him my wallet.

I can't really remember saying much back, but as he moved his right hand, possibly to get his knife out, I stood up and grabbed his head under the chin and pushed his head back, pushing him towards the back of the bus. I did a sort of osoto gari, but with no reap as there wasn't enough room really. All I could concentrate on was pushing his head into the floor of the bus. His mate took a swing at me with his leg, which I managed to block or parry as if going for a ko uchi gari from a kick, but instead I just kicked him as hard as I could between the legs and he dropped like a stone.

I could hear some commotion from the back of the bus and in my rage I considered going up there and taking them all on, though I don't think I would have lasted long. I turned and started running down the stairs. I think someone caught me on the back of the head with a punch or something but with the adrenaline I can't remember really feeling anything.

Luckily by this time the bus had arrived at my stop and I managed to escape. As the bus pulled off, they threw my Walkman out the window and it smashed all over the ground. I was still extremely angry but still, I consider myself quite lucky to have got away without serious injury.

Jaime

# CHAPTER **FOUR** green belt

By the time you have passed your orange belt you will have begun to understand about the process of learning Jiu Jitsu techniques and applying the techniques. At green belt you start to focus on the intent you need in order to use the techniques quickly and effectively.

## EMBU

In Jiu Jitsu embu refers to working co-operatively and harmoniously with another Jiu Jitsuka in a way that is more than simple training. The training starts to develop into something that could be considered more spiritual – the Jiu Jitsuka share the dojo and the atmosphere of the dojo with each other. The techniques they use don't just affect the Jiu Jitsuka practising them but everyone else in the dojo as well. The techniques and application of the techniques are in total harmony and each movement performed by the tori and uke exemplifies the concept of cutting away from and reconnecting with each other. Embu in the dojo is far removed from the use of Jiu Jitsu in real life situations where the Jiu Jitsuka has no need for emotional involvement with their attacker.

The green belt is often seen as one of the most difficult grades to pass in Jiu Jitsu as you have to be able to prove to yourself and your instructors that you are capable of looking after your uke in physically demanding and potentially dangerous training situations as well as protecting yourself using basic Jiu Jitsu techniques in real life situations.

Warm-ups should always include groundwork and back-to-back fighting where Jiu Jitsuka compete against each other to hold each other on the ground using the holds you have already learned. As you progress through Jiu Jitsu you will also learn to use joint locks and strangles in ground fighting.

At green belt, students also start to develop an understanding of embu.

## Traditional techniques
### ADVANCED UKEMI

As you return to the standing ukemi kata at the start of every session start thinking about ukemi not only as a means of avoiding serious harm when thrown or of a way to distance yourself from an opponent. Practise the ukemi kata as a

*Start by projecting yourself over a partner crouching on the floor*

*To responding to a strong push from behind*

*To a partner bent at the waist*

series of interconnected moves that gracefully harmonise and synchronise your breathing, movement and momentum.

Focus on the circular movement in each part of the ukemi.

Each part of the ukemi kata can be used at different levels.

Notice the difference between a novice's forward roll and a forward roll performed by a green belt.

*Novice forward roll*

*From height*

*Green belt forward roll*

*Novice backward roll*

Progressions in ukemi should also be obvious in backward rolls.

It is vitally important to keep your head tucked in when you fall backwards from height. Remember to breathe out as you hit the ground.

*And in style*

## ATEMI WAZA

### *Ushiro geri – rear kick*

Ushiro geri is used to strike when being attacked from the rear. Begin by standing in a parallel stance, feet shoulder-width apart. First look over your shoulder at your uke, then thrust your heel towards your target as quickly and powerfully as you can. Your foot should be heel forwards with your toes pointing downwards. The striking surface is the heel of your foot.

### *Mawashi geri – roundhouse kick*

Although mawashi geri is one of the most popular kicks in Jiu Jitsu it is difficult to perform well. You have already studied the basic kick at orange belt but further work will be needed if you are to perform the kick properly at green belt.

When performed correctly, mawashi geri can be devastatingly fast and effective in strikes to the

**TRAINING TIP**

The kick can be used to attack at any level from the knee to the head but Jiu Jitsuka should focus on aiming for vulnerable areas below the chest.

ribs, kidney, solar plexus, groin, knees and shins. Many attacks can be ended quickly as a result of a good mawashi geri to the knee.

Begin by standing in a yoi stance. A strong stance is particularly important for a good kick as you must have a stable platform from which to launch your kick.

Propel your knee forwards by using your toes and heel like a spring. Once your knee points at the target, snap your leg forwards from the knee. You can give the kick power by rotating your hip and your support leg. Strike your uke target with the ball of the foot in training but with the end or instep of your shoe in real life situations.

Practise your roundhouse kicks low until you perfect them before you attempt the higher kicks.

## KANSETZU WAZA

One good reason for learning how to put arm locks on is so that you can learn how to get out of them.

The secret to countering arm locks is to react quickly and to use atemi strikes to vulnerable parts of the body immediately before you apply the counters.

### Counter to first arm lock from the outside

As your uke applies the first arm lock to your right arm from the outside, strike across your uke's face and take hold of your right wrist with your left hand.

127

Bend your right arm and continue to push your bent arm back into your uke. As you feel your uke's centre of balance move backwards take your uke to the ground with kosoto gake.

Don't forget to finish off your uke.

### Counter to first arm lock from the inside

As your uke applies the first arm lock to your right arm from the inside, drive your left knee into your uke's groin and reach over to take hold of your right wrist with your left hand.

Step back and around with your left leg, pivoting on your right foot. Pull back sharply on your right arm and into the fifth arm lock, keeping upwards pressure on the lower and upper arm until the arm lock is fully applied.

### Counter to second arm lock

As your uke starts to apply the second arm lock on your right arm, take hold of their left arm with your left arm.

As you quickly and forcefully step in front of your uke, extend their right arm across your body. Continue your forward movement and throw your weight onto your uke's elbow so that you have reversed the arm lock.

129

Jump up and around your uke, pushing down on their shoulder at the same time to relieve pressure on your locked arm. As you come down, stamp down on the back of your uke's left leg using kosoto gake to take them to the ground.

Follow your uke to the ground and finish off.

**TRAINING TIP**

In training it is very important to let go of your uke's wrist as you apply pressure at the elbow to avoid injury to the elbow joint. You should never practise this technique without letting go of the elbow.

*Counter to second arm lock for a taller person*

As your uke starts to apply the second arm lock for a taller person on your right arm, turn into your uke and place your left hand onto their left shoulder.

arm lock, taking hold of your right wrist with your left hand.

Keep moving forwards quickly through the lock, using your body weight and momentum to free your arm.

Turn back into your uke and take them to the floor by pulling sharply on their hair or using kosoto gari.

## Counter to third arm lock

As your uke starts to apply the third arm lock on your right arm, push forwards and against the

## Ground immobilisations using arm and wrist locks

Joint locks are also used to control your uke on the ground. Practise moving smoothly and quickly from lock to lock but remember that in real life situations you usually will only have to apply one lock to control your attacker. The power behind the locks comes mainly from your body

*Side knee arm lock – yoko hiza gatame*

*Side arm entanglement – Yoko ude garami*

*Side wrist trap – yoko koto dori*

*Rear hand twist – ura kote gaeshi*

*Rear knee arm lock – Ura hiza gatame*

*Leg triangle entanglement – ashi sangaku garami*

positioning and the momentum you create as you apply the locks, not from using body strength. In training, ask your uke to try to resist the application of a lock and, as they resist, counter their lines of resistance to find the position in which they are most vulnerable. If you can't apply one lock because of your uke's resistance try to apply another instead.

## NAGE WAZA

At green belt, throws are either performed as one smooth movement from initial attack to take down and finish off, or as throws where the tori has to work really hard to generate the momentum for the throw to work effectively. At first, practise each throw slowly and do not build up speed until you feel you have understood the technique properly.

### Harai goshi – sweeping hip

You must try to keep your uke moving throughout this throw.

Move to the inside of the attack, leading with your right leg. Parry your uke's right hand roundhouse punch with your left hand. As you keep moving, your right hand moves in a circle under your uke's left arm.

133

Lean forwards and take your uke's weight onto your left foot. As you feel your uke's balance transfer forwards, drive your right arm up to lift your uke and as their feet start to leave the ground sweep back with your right leg at hip height.

Pivot on your right foot until your hips are almost parallel with your uke's hips. Your left foot should be about 12 inches in front of your right.

Keep driving your right arm up and pull around with your left arm. If you have used kuzushi effectively and kept your uke moving then they should flip over your leg and onto their back.

Finish off with atemi strikes as your uke hits the ground.

### *Tsurikomi goshi – lifting pulling hip*

Again you must try to keep your uke moving throughout this throw.

As your uke tries to grab you with both hands and push you backwards, move to the inside of the attack, leading with your right leg. Take hold of your uke at the right wrist and under their left armpit.

Simultaneously drive your uke's right arm down and the left arm up as you step into the attack, pivoting on your right foot. Try to strike your uke with your right elbow as you step in. Keep pivoting on your right foot until your hips are parallel with your uke's hips. Continue to pull down and around with your left arm and drive up with your right arm.

Drop right under your uke to take their weight. As you feel your uke's balance transfer forwards, drive up and over with your right arm up to lift them and as their weight transfers onto your hips pull around with your left arm.

Keep driving your right arm up and pull around with your left arm. If you have used kuzushi effectively and kept your uke moving they will flip over your hips and onto their back. Finish off with atemi strikes as your uke hits the ground.

135

Irimi nage emphasises the importance of embu – synchronising and harmonising every aspect of your movement with that of your uke.

## Irimi nage – entering body throw

Perhaps more than any other throw, irimi nage shows why it is so important to keep your uke moving and not throw from a static position. Practise irimi nage slowly and smoothly. Only speed up when you are confident that you understand the technique. From start to finish a successful irimi nage will take less than a second.

As your uke punches with a right straight punch, step to the outside, leading with your left foot. Parry the strike with your right arm.

Simultaneously bring your left arm around to strike your uke with the heel of your left hand at the base of the neck, driving them forwards in the direction of their punch.

Pivot on your right foot, stepping into your uke with your left foot. As you do, slide your left arm around your uke's neck, pushing forwards and around. Your right arm drops over your uke's right arm; pull the arm towards you and now start to pivot away from your uke, completely reversing the entering movement you have just made. As you do that, catch your uke's chin with your left hand, pull backwards and around and drive the upper part of your right arm into their head in a circular movement.

Complete pivoting out, leading with your left leg. Keep driving your right arm around and pull around with your left arm. As you feel your uke start to lose balance, pull down on the chin and push around and down with your right arm. If you have used kuzushi effectively and kept your uke moving, they will fall onto their side. Finish off with an arm lock and atemi strike.

### Tai otoshi – body drop

You will need to learn to use tai otoshi in two ways, first from a parry and secondly a block.

### Tai otoshi from a parry

From a right roundhouse punch move to the inside of your attacker, leading with your right leg. Parry the punch with both arms and take hold of the upper arm. Don't stop your uke's momentum.

**TRAINING TIP**
You are aiming to place your right foot midway between your uke's feet.

Keep turning on your right foot and as you twist into your uke bring your left foot forwards. Keep twisting until you are facing the same way as your uke and your hips are parallel with theirs.

Swing your arms across in front of you as if you were cutting corn with a scythe. Your right leg moves to the outside of your uke's legs, your right knee slightly bent.

Drop right under your uke to take their weight. Continue to drive your arms across your body. As you feel your uke's balance transfer forwards and onto your right leg, straighten your leg to give them something to fall over.

Keep driving your arms across your body. If you have used kuzushi effectively and kept your uke moving, they will flip over your hip and leg and onto their back. Finish off with atemi strikes as your uke hits the ground.

### Tai otoshi from a block

Take up a migi yoi – right-sided ready stance. From a right roundhouse punch swing both arms with a whipping action into the punch to block and stop the punch. Generate movement from your hips to increase the force behind the block.

**TRAINING TIP**

Block with the sides of your hand. In real life situations you are attempting to break your attacker's arms with the force of your block.

Drop your blocking arms over your uke's right arm and, pivoting on your right foot, twist into your uke, pulling their arms as hard as you can across your body. As you twist you will find that you have to step in with your left leg to keep your balance. Keep twisting until you are facing the same way as your uke and your hips are parallel with theirs.

139

Swing your arms across in front of you as if you were cutting corn with a scythe. Your right leg will be to the outside of your uke's legs, your right knee slightly bent.

Drop right under your uke to take their weight. Continue to drive your arms across your body. As you feel your uke's balance transfer forwards and onto your right leg, straighten your leg to give them something to fall over.

Keep driving your arms across your body. If you have used kuzushi effectively and kept your uke moving, they will flip over your hip and leg and onto their back.

### Uki goshi – floating hip
Block across your body with your right hand to stop your uke's close-quarter right-hand punch to your face. As you block, step to the inside of the attack, leading with your right leg.

The blocking arm continues in a semi-circle under your uke's left arm. Your left arm pulls their right forearm tightly towards your body and your right hip is now lined up with the right side of your uke's groin.

Simultaneously drive your right hip into the right side of their groin.

As you lift with your right arm, pull around with your left. It will take some time to co-ordinate all these movements at the same time. As you feel

your uke's balance transfer backwards, pull even harder with your left arm.

If you have used kuzushi effectively then they should fall over your hip and onto their side.

### Tani otoshi – valley drop

As your uke punches with a right straight punch, step to the outside and directly behind them, leading with your left foot. Parry the strike with your right arm and strike your uke in the face with your left.

Simultaneously drive backwards with your left elbow into your uke's throat and hook your right arm under their right leg.

As your uke starts to lose their balance lift their right leg off the ground and backwards over your legs.

If you have used sufficient force and broken balance correctly then your uke will fall backwards over your legs. Finish off with a series of atemi strikes.

Now reverse all the instructions and practise every throw on the other side.

**TRAINING TIP**
Your left leg needs to be directly behind both of your uke's legs.

## OSAEKOMI WAZA

By now you will have become used to using a small number of groundwork techniques and will have practised them in ground fighting and back-to-back sessions. Because you understand the principles behind the holds, you should find the green belt techniques easy to pick up.

As with all the other techniques, start slowly and build up speed but don't be afraid to get stuck in when you practise. Don't let go until your uke taps out, and do be very aware of what else is happening on the mat. If you are too close to other Jiu Jitsuka then stop and find more space.

### Starting point

As you start practising use the traditional grip you learned for orange belt but as soon as you feel comfortable with the hold downs practise them from a gentle ground-fighting position – ask your uke to resist the hold downs but not too much! Again ask your uke to try to escape or land effective strikes to your body. Find good positions to minimise your uke's movement. Practise with as many different uke as possible as there will always be differences in how you use the ground-holds depending on the size, stature and weight of the uke.

### Ushiro yoko shiho gatame – reverse side four-quarters hold

Position your back between your uke's stomach and chest, so that you are literally lying on them.

Your left arm goes in between your attacker's legs and grips the leg nearest you. Your right arm goes over and under your uke's head. Ask your uke to shift their balance and experiment with your legs in, with knees touching your uke's body, or out.

### Kami shiho gatame – upper four-quarters hold

Your chest needs to be on your uke's chest, your arms under your uke's arms. Press down hard to resist their movement and experiment with leg positioning and moving points of contact and balance.

### tate shiho gatame – lower four-quarters hold

Look for chest-to-chest contact with one arm around your uke's neck, the other to help you keep balance. Press down hard to resist your uke's movement and experiment with leg positioning and moving points of contact and balance. Ask your uke to arch their back and feel the difference when you wrap your legs under their body.

You can use a headlock at the same time by pushing your right shoulder under your uke's chin and levering their head backwards. You must let go as soon as your uke taps.

### *Mune gatame – chest hold*

Gather and trap your uke's arms into the side of their body with your arms and knees. Chest to chest contact is important.

Now try everything on the other side!

# Self-defence

As you reach the end of the beginner's stage of Jiu Jitsu great importance is placed on being able to use the techniques you have learned so far in a self-defence situation. Use common sense to pick the techniques that work for you – it's no good trying to throw an attacker in koshi guruma if you can't even reach their neck. Always use substance over style: something might look good but does it actually work? If you find yourself sud-

denly using techniques that you hadn't planned and they work, then congratulations. You've started to act intuitively and you're well on your way to getting to grips with Jiu Jitsu.

## KEEPING ATTACKERS AT A DISTANCE

Use atemi waza to keep one attacker away from you. Combine strikes to the face and vulnerable parts of the body with kicks to the lower part of the body to create distance between you and your attacker. In every case try to stand your ground against your attacker but don't trade punches or kicks with them. Practise each technique slowly, building up speed as you become more confident.

### *Open hand strike to the ear*

Block across your body from the outside. Strike open handed to the ear.

### TRAINING TIP

In training pull your strike, as you could burst your uke's ear drum.

## Slap to face

Block across your body from the outside and slap your attacker's face.

### TRAINING TIP

Get used to physical contact. In real life you are going to have to hit your attacker hard.

## Strike to the groin

Block across your body from the outside and drop to strike your attacker in the groin.

## Yoko geri to the kneecap

Although you are aiming to break your attacker's knee in training you must ensure that you do not follow through with the kick or use maximum force.

As your attacker punches, simultaneously drop and block, targeting the knee using yoko geri.

## Ushiro geri to the groin

As your attacker comes up behind you, look to see who it is (it might be a friend!), drop leaning forwards and target the groin using ushiro geri.

## PRACTICAL APPLICATIONS OF NAGE WAZA

Each of the throws you have learned for green belt can now be used in self-defence.

### Harai goshi – sweeping hip

Against a roundhouse attack with a bottle or cosh, step inside the arc of the attack and parry the arm holding the weapon.

147

1.

2.

3.

4.

You must disarm your attacker of the weapons once they have hit the ground.

Finish off with atemi strikes to vulnerable parts of the body.

1.

## Irimi nage – entering body throw

Against a backhand attack from a bottle or cosh, parry the arm holding the weapon and move with the attack.

2.

1.

3.

You must disarm your attacker of the weapons once they have hit the ground.

Finish off with atemi strikes to vulnerable parts of the body.

> **TRAINING TIP**
>
> Make sure you have plenty of space around you when you practise weapons defences as weapons may fly out of your attacker's hand when you parry or block the arm holding the weapon.

### Tsurikomi goshi – lifting pulling hip

Against a naked neck strangle, strike down hard on one arm and push up on the other and strike to the chin as you gather in your attacker's right arm.

Use tsurikomi goshi to throw your attacker.

Finish off with atemi strikes to vulnerable parts of the body.

Start to build up defensive speed against a series of body grabs using the following techniques.

### Tai otoshi – body drop

Against an overarm body grab from behind, throw your head backwards, targeting your attacker's nose as you drop, and force your arms out to the front.

Take a firm grip of one arm and throw your attacker in tai otoshi.

### *Uki goshi – floating hip*

Against an over arm body grab from the front, head-butt your attacker and strike to the groin.

Step into your attacker, throwing them using uki goshi (see over).

*Uki goshi*

### Tani Otoshi – valley drop

Against an overarm body grab from the side, grab your attacker's groin and stamp on their toes.

Step behind your attacker and push them back over your left leg, throwing them using tani otoshi.

**TRAINING TIP**

To begin with, practise each defence individually. As soon as you have mastered each defence start practising in groups of four – yourself and three opponents. Keep moving between attacks and don't give your opponents the upper hand. It's essential to finish each opponent quickly so don't try to lock them or pin them to the ground as it takes too much time. Use atemi strikes to vulnerable parts of the body instead. Don't worry if your defences feel messy – you're looking for effectiveness, not grace and beauty, in each defence.

## ADVANCED DEFENCES AGAINST HEAD GRABS

An advanced combination of strikes to vulnerable parts of the body, throws and locks are very effective against head grabs.

### Hair grabs – front

Sweep over your uke's arms and strike with your right hand to their neck.

2.

1.

Step in as you strike with your right leg and drive your body into your uke's side. As you feel their grip loosen follow through into osotogari.

3.

Follow your uke to the floor and use atemi strikes to finish off.

153

### Hair grabs – back

Strike down on one of your uke's arms and strike with your right fist to their neck to loosen their grip on your hair.

Drive back into your uke's side. As you feel their grip loosen follow through into ouchi gari.

Follow your uke to the floor and use atemi strikes to the groin to finish off.

### Naked strangle – front

Drive up between your uke's arms to loosen their grip on your throat and bring both arms down onto their collarbone.

**TRAINING TIP**

Try to force your chin to your chest to protect your throat and breathe out sharply as you drive your arms up to protect your windpipe. Using a kiai will help.

1.

Step into your uke and pivot on your right foot into them. Drop under them and use koshi guruma to throw them over your hip.

2.

Follow your uke to the floor and use atemi strikes to finish off.

### Naked strangle – back

Stamp on your uke's toes. Start to turn into them, striking the groin as you turn. Push down as hard as you can on their thumb as you turn and try to break it by forcing it down onto the back of your neck.

Continue turning right under your uke's arm until you are facing them. Strike to their nose using your right elbow and follow through into osoto gari to take your uke to the ground.

1.

Follow your uke to the floor and use atemi strikes to finish off.

2.

### Two-hand to two-hand grab

Attackers who grab hold of both your hands and confront you face on are generally very confident of the outcome of their attack. They have actually put themselves in an incredibly vulnerable position by exposing their legs and groin to kicks, and their head and face head butts.

As your uke grabs both your wrists, bend your arms at the elbow and push down into your attacker's grabs – don't try to pull away from them.

As they start to resist, open and rotate your hands inwards to bring your palms up to face you. You will find this easy to do as long as you have bent your arms.

Now turn your wrists slightly so the narrow part of your wrists is lined up with the gap between your uke's fingers and thumbs. Pull your arms back sharply towards you, stepping backwards at the same time, using your momentum against their strength.

Step back in to strike your uke on the carotids with both hands. You can take your uke to the ground using ashi guruma.

## TRUE STORY: YOU'RE NEVER TOO OLD

I gave up Jiu Jitsu last summer because I knew it was getting a bit much for me, with so much emphasis in my club on grading. But I did get to green belt and still feel an immense pride and satisfaction in achieving that.

I took up Jitsu aged 46 almost by mistake while trying to encourage my teenaged sons to do it, and while suffering from a slipped disc and asthma. I then added a broken thumb (yellow grading) and an ACL knee injury from which I recovered to take my orange and then finally green. I got so much from my time on the mat and am so grateful for the experience. It really was about personal development. The fact that I was accepted as an equal by people more than half my age and had such fun along the way was an exceptional bonus. The friends I made on the mat are still in touch and some of them look set to be friends for life. I owe a huge personal debt to Jitsu for this.

Amanda

## AN INTRODUCTION TO WORKING WITH KNIVES AND BROKEN BOTTLES

Kansetzu waza – joint locking techniques – can be used against many attacks with imitation and real sharp weapons. However, before you start practising against even imitation knives and broken bottles at green belt there are a few simple rules that you must always follow.

### Safety rules

1 For green belt start practising with blunt wooden imitation knives and plastic bottles, and only move on to more 'realistic' weapons when you feel comfortable.

2 Do not practise with real weapons until you have been awarded your purple belt and are supervised by an experienced and qualified instructor. You can still have a lot of fun and learn a lot by practising with imitation weapons.

3 Never practise with real weapons unless there is sufficient safety space on the mat.

4 Never practise real weapons defences with a green belt or below.

5 Always keep your fingers in when you block.

6 No matter how good you are you will almost certainly be cut when you practise with sharp weapons so have a good first aid kit and make sure your instructor knows how to use it.

7 Train with each other, not against each other. If as an uke you notice that your partner freezes **do not continue your attack**.

8 Remember the tapping out rule when you disarm your uke in practice.

9 Take extra care when you disarm an uke in training.

10 Never use the weapon on the uke once you have disarmed them.

> **TRAINING TIP**
>
> Don't hurry any of these techniques as they will take time to learn effectively, even though you will already know the joint locks. It is critically important to practise the weapon disarms precisely. Always imagine that you are practising against a real weapon – if you touch any sharp part of an imitation weapon in practice then you have got the technique wrong. In real life you would have been cut!

### Common sense

There is no doubt that sharp weapons can be really scary, especially if you are just about to be attacked by somebody holding one. That is why you must always start practising with wooden or rubber knives and plastic broken bottles before you get anywhere close to a real weapon.

If you are threatened with a real sharp weapon but not stabbed, then you should always use physical defence as an absolute last resort. Many attackers will use sharp weapons 'functionally'.

They want something from you and threatening you with a sharp weapon will produce the results. Unless it's something you really can't give them, then give in. Belongings can be replaced, you can't.

## Psychological preparation

At other times you will have no choice; you will have to defend yourself. In these situations psychological preparation is essential and just as important as physical preparation. Your heart will be beating hard and your breathing may become laboured – you need to exert control over your body. Focus on your own skills and the fact that you know something your attacker doesn't. You have the element of surprise, you are a Jiu Jitsuka and you have practised defences against weapons. You have a key choice to make – you can assert control over your attacker by taking up a solid yoi stance, standing your ground, remaining totally silent and being prepared to spring at your attacker as soon as you see an opening. It will almost seem as if you are goading your attacker to attack you. You are going to match your movement to theirs, constantly looking for the opening you need to defend yourself. Alternatively you can pretend to back away, giving your attacker the impression that they are totally in control of the situation. Let them feel confident, that they have nothing to be afraid of, and then at the moment of attack change from soft to hard.

In some situations you will have very little warning that you are going to be attacked or the attack is incredibly fast and unpredictable. In both cases remember the golden rule – keep your hands up, fingers in and arms away from your body. Ask training partners to attack you with wooden knives and plastic broken bottles and practise getting out of the way. Ask your training partner to vary their attacks, to be unpredictable, keep looking for openings. To begin with you will be caught many times but you need to sharpen your reflexes. Even black belts will get caught but not as much as you.

## Attack: knife/broken bottle attack to the face

## Defence: second arm lock – karada gatame – body lock

Parry the right-handed broken bottle attack to your face while stepping to the outside of your uke, leading with your left foot.

159

As your uke's arm moves past your face, slide your right hand down towards their fist and grasp their wrist firmly with your right hand.

Keep pressure on the arm until your uke has released the broken bottle.

Simultaneously step through with your left leg and strike to the face with your left hand. Continuing your forward movement, throw your weight onto your uke's right elbow and use the second arm lock – karada gatame – to lock the arm.

### TRAINING TIP

Remember that in training you must let go of your uke's wrist as you 'snap' on the arm lock to avoid accidentally breaking your partner's arm.

*Attack: downward knife attack to the upper body*

*Defence: third arm lock – jodan ude garami – upper body arm entanglement*
Block a downward right-handed knife attack with your left arm held at a right angle, and your body aligned to support the block.

Immediately bring your right arm up and under your uke's right arm to support your left arm. Your right hand should be over your left hand. Bring your elbows together, making sure that the knife is held away from your face.

Step through with your right leg, levering your uke's arm backwards as you move past your attacker.

Continue stepping through and levering the arm backwards until your uke has to fall to protect their arm from breaking. Keep the lock on until your uke has let go of the knife.

### Attack: Knife/broken bottle attack to the stomach

### Defence: Second wrist lock – ura kote – reverse twist

Use a cross block to block a right-handed knife attack to the stomach. Remember that your right hand must be over your left hand.

**TRAINING TIP**
Change your hands over for a left-hand attack.

As your uke starts to bend, use downward pressure on their wrist to apply the wrist lock. You should apply the pressure immediately, not gradually. Finish with a right-foot mae geri kick to your uke's face.

Kick to your uke's knee and take a firm hold of their right arm just above the wrist. Sharply turn your uke's arm and wrist clockwise and at the same time step back sharply with your right leg.

Keep applying pressure on the wrist until your uke has let go of the knife.

The technique is reversed if you are defending yourself against a left-sided attack.

### Attack: knife/broken bottle attack to the stomach

### Defence: fifth arm lock – hiji gatame – elbow lock

Again it is essential to use a hard block to stop your uke as they aim to strike your stomach or groin with a knife or broken bottle. Use a whipping movement to your uke's wrist as you use a cross block to stop the attack at least 12 inches from your body.

As soon as you have stopped your uke's movement, take hold of their wrist with your top hand and start to rotate their arm clockwise.

As their arm reaches the highest point, push down sharply on the elbow, making sure you avoid contact with the knife.

way outside of an attacker's hitting range or all the way inside. Your attacker either can't reach you or can't punch into themselves sufficiently hard to do you any real damage.

In most unarmed attacks, and especially those which are a general brawl, the rule is therefore to get in as close as you can. Close the distance between yourself and your attacker as quickly and as safely as you can. Don't trade punches or kicks as, often, an attacker is surprised when you close with him instead of backing off, which is what most people do when attacked.

As your attacker starts to throw right- and left-hand punches at you, get your hands up to your forehead with your forearms in a vertical wedge shape protecting your face. Your fists should be

Draw out the arm and keep pressure on the elbow. Use chest pressure to keep the arm lock on and do not relax until your uke has dropped their weapon. Take them to the floor by pulling back on their head and using kosoto gake.

## FIGHTING TO THE GROUND

### Getting started

The most dangerous distance in any unarmed altercation against a single attacker is when you are within kicking and punching range. Unfortunately, most social interaction, whether it is positive or negative, is done within punching distance where you are most likely to be caught. As a Jiu Jitsuka you will either want to be all the

tightly locked against your forehead and your elbows leading forwards, protecting your face against the punches.

As you quickly move into your attacker, aim fast, short kicks to their knees and shins – no higher or you may lose your balance. Don't worry if the kicks are messy – this whole defence will feel messy to begin with! As you close the distance, sweep your hands out as though you are swimming the breaststroke to block both of your uke's biceps on each arm. Trap your uke's arms by hooking your hands over their upper arms and using your forearms to control their arms.

You should have your forehead tight against your attacker's chest while hooking over the back of their upper forearms. Use the tension you are

generating by pulling in on your attacker's arms and pushing with your head against their chest to limit their punching and movement. Now, complete the hold by reaching around your attacker's back with either your right or left arm and moving to that side. Trap your attacker's other arm tightly under your armpit. You can protect your face more by burying it into the upper part of your attacker's trapped arm.

Try to lock your thighs around whichever of your attacker's legs is closest to you. This will limit their ability to turn and knee you in the groin.

To take your attacker to the floor, continue to move under your attacker's arm until you are behind them. Keep tight hold around the waist and keep your head in to avoid any elbow strikes targeted at your face. Your head should now be pushed into their back.

You should now have some control over your attacker even if they are still trying to punch you. You will also notice that your attacker is now also trying to shake you off.

### TRAINING TIP

In training, check your points of contact with your uke. Your head should be against your uke's chest, one arm around their waist, which you can secure by holding their clothing. Feel the difference in control when you let go of your uke with this arm. Use your other arm to trap your uke's arm under your armpit and hold the back of their elbow to use it as a shield for your face. Finally, make sure you are controlling your uke's leg closest to you to limit their movement and protect against a knee to the groin.

Move your foot out and block your attacker's far foot – on the right side your right foot steps out to the right to block behind your attacker's right heel. Now sit down to drag your attacker to the ground, tripping them over your outstretched leg. If you have done the take down correctly your attacker will not be able to keep their balance because you are blocking their foot and stopping them from stepping back. Again don't worry if it looks and feels messy.

As soon as your attacker hits the floor hold them down using any of the locks or ground holds you have already learned. The choice is yours.

**TRUE STORY: THE WORST GRADING OF MY LIFE**

After training for about 15 months my instructor put me in for my green belt. I thought it would be as easy as my first two belts, which I'd sailed through because I already did judo and karate and thought I was pretty tough. It was really different to how I'd expected though. I could do the technical stuff. My instructor had already told me that there was an emphasis on self-defence at green belt but the speed and unpredictability of some of the attacks really shocked me. I consider myself to be physically fit but I learned that Jiu Jitsu was far more about preparing yourself mentally for unpredictable situations than being able to stand in the middle and take a punch.

I only just scraped through the grading and a lot of the smaller students were better than me, even though they weren't as strong or fit, because they had a much better awareness of what was going on and were able to adjust their defences to the attacks. I just kept trying to do the same thing even when it was obviously going wrong. At the end the examiner took me aside and asked me what had gone wrong – the truth was I thought that because I could do the techniques I would be able to defend myself. I've realised that Jiu Jitsu is very different from a lot of other martial arts where all you do is learn the techniques. In Jiu Jitsu it's more important to know how to apply them in real situations that are unpredictable and messy. I've done two more gradings now but I won't forget the lessons I learned at green belt.

Paul

# CHAPTER **FIVE** the next steps

By now you will have been training in Jiu Jitsu for at least 18 months and will have started to develop a good understanding of what Jiu Jitsu is all about. You've done very well to come this far but there is still a long way to go until you get to black belt. Don't fall into the trap and think you know it all – you don't. Lower grades will start to look up to you and you need to be a good role model. It's fine to be confident and assertive; it's not OK to be arrogant and aggressive. Keep hold of the humility and respect that you show in the dojo and try not to lose sight of who you really are.

Good luck in your future training.

David Walker

# Glossary

## A

- Aerobic warm-up exercises – exercises that use oxygen in the process of generating energy, are of moderate intensity and are undertaken for a long duration

- Anaerobic warm-up exercises – exercises used to build power, and by bodybuilders to build muscle mass, but not to develop or increase stamina. Useful for short duration–high-intensity activities

- Ashi sangaku garami – leg triangle entanglement – 5th leglock

- Atemi – strikes or kicks to vulnerable areas of the head or body

- Atemi Waza – striking techniques

## B

- Blocks – hard and fast movements with the hands or feet with the intention of stopping movement and causing damage

- Brazilian Jiu Jitsu – an offshoot of Japanese Jiu Jitsu that has been systematically and progressively developed in Brazil for use primarily in mixed martial arts competition. Brazilian Jiu Jitsu is a very popular and highly successful style of competitive Jiu Jitsu in its own right. Heavy emphasis on ground fighting

- British Ju Jitsu Association (GB) – nationally recognised umbrella organisation for several different styles of Jiu Jitsu in the UK (note different spelling)

- Bushido – the 'way of the warrior'. The Japanese military code of behaviour developed in feudal times to support range of fighting arts and skills (Bujitsu) studied by the Samurai

## C

- Countering – techniques used to oppose an attacker who has knowledge of locking, strangling, striking and throwing systems

## D

- Dachi – stance

- Dan grade – grade, as from black belt, indicating a basic mastery of the martial art

- Dangerous parts kata – pattern of atemi strikes targeting vulnerable areas on the head, and front and back of body

- Do – way

- Dojo – training hall – literally 'place of the way'

- Drop – a method of falling safely on to your front whilst protecting face and body from injury

## E

- Embu – in Jiu Jitsu 'embu' refers to working co-operatively and harmoniously with another Jiu Jitsuka to capture the 'spirit' of the art

## F

- Finishing off – every defensive skill is completed with a locking, striking or choking/strangling technique that renders an uke or attacker unwilling or unable to continue aggressive movement towards you

- Fish hook – the application of pressure on the inner cheek following the placement of one or two fingers inside the mouth of an attacker between the jaw and inner cheek

## G

- Gedan ude garami – lower level arm entanglement – 4th arm lock

- Gi – see keikogi

- Green belt – 5th kyu

- Ground immobilisations – any technique allowing an uke or attacker to be held or tapped on the ground

- Groundwork – any technique that is used on an uke or attacker on the ground

## H

- Harai goshi – sweeping hip

- Hidari – left

- Hiji Gatame – elbow lock – 5th arm lock

- Hiza Geri – knee kick – very powerful close-quarter technique mainly used to attack the groin, stomach or head

## I

- Ippon Seoi Nage – single-point shoulder throw or one-arm shoulder throw in Shorinji Kan Jiu Jitsu

- Irimi nage – entering body throw

## J

- Jigaro Kano – a master of Jiu Jitsu and the founder of modern Judo

- Jitsu – the art or technique

- Jitsu Foundation – one of the largest schools of Jiu Jitsu in the United Kingdom

- Jiu Jitsu – technique or art of suppleness, flexibility and gentleness

- Jiu Jitsuka – student(s) of Jiu Jitsu

- Jodan Ude Garami – upper body arm entanglement – 3rd arm lock

- Ju (Jiu) – at its most literal, meaning gentle, soft or flexible

- Judo – literally 'yielding way'. Founded by Jigaro Kano as the 'perfect form of Jiu Jitsu'. There are no kicks, strikes, or wrist-locks, leg-locks and headlocks in Judo

- Judoka – student of Judo

## K

- Kami Shiho Gatame – upper four-quarters hold

- Kannuki gatame – inside straight-arm bolt lock – alternative 1st arm lock

- Kansetzu waza (alt. spelling is kensetsu waza) – joint-locking techniques of any of the body joints

- Karada Gatame – body lock – 2nd armlock

- Karate – Okinawan/Japanese martial arts primarily involving kicks and punches. Literally 'empty hand'

- Kata – a set pattern of moves in Japanese martial arts

- Kata Gatame – shoulder hold

- Kata g(a)uruma – shoulder wheel

- Katana – Japanese long sword, single-edged blade, 24–36 inches long

- Katsugi Gatame – tall person shoulder carry lock – alternative 2nd armlock

- Keikogi – usually referred to simply as a gi, clothing used to practice Jiu Jitsu

- Kenset(s)zu Waza – see Kansetzu Waza

- Keza Gatame – Scarf hold (alt. spellings are kesa gatame, kessa gatame)

- Kiai – name given to a short yell that Jiu Jitsuka shout before or during a fight or technique. Literally 'heavenly scream', helps tighten body muscles before countering an attack

- Kiba dachi – horseriding stance

- Koshi g(a)uruma – hip wheel

- kosoto gake – minor outer hook

- Kosoto gari – minor outer reap

- Kote gaeshi – outside wrist twist – 1st wrist lock

- Koto gatame – inner wrist lock – 3rd wrist lock

- Kujiki gatame – outside arm break – 1st arm lock

- Kung fu – generic name used for martial arts of Chinese origin

- Kuzushi – term used for breaking an attacker's stability or unbalancing them in some way. Also used 'to destroy'

- Kyu grades – student grades in Jiu Jitsu below black belt

## M

- Ma ai – the use of distance between you and your attacker
- Mae geri – front kick
- Mae ukemi – forward breakfall
- Matae – stop
- Mawashi geri – roundhouse kick
- Mawashi hiza geri – roundhouse knee kick and a very powerful close quarter technique mainly used to attack the groin, stomach
- Migi – right
- Mokusou – a period of contemplation
- Mons – a pass (no mons), a good pass (1 mon), an excellent pass (2 mon) or an exceptional pass (3 mon)
- Mune gatame – chest hold
- Mushin – mind of no mind. Acting (intuitively) without thinking

## N

- Nage Waza – throwing techniques
- Ni dan – 2nd dan (a 2nd dan in one style may have actually trained longer and harder and have more experience than a higher dan in another style)

## O

- Obi – belt
- O goshi – major hip throw
- O uchi gari – major inner reap from punch and kick
- Orange belt – 6th kyu
- Osaekomi waza – groundwork techniques
- Osoto gari – major outer reaping throw
- otagi ni rei – 'I return the bow'

- Over the belt – falling technique designed to improve yoko ukemi (side falling) techniques

## P

- Parries – firm and protective arm or leg movements with the intention to deflect the attack yet still allow the uke or attacker's movement
- Peg leg breakfall – left and right falling technique designed to improve yoko ukemi (side falling)

## R

- Rei – name given to the traditional Japanese bow or salutation

## S

- Samurai – Japanese feudal knight/warrior. Samurai were trained in a wide variety of martial arts practices
- Self-defence – any martial art may be used for self-protection, but actions used in self-defence must be consistent with the legal system of the country they are used in
- Sensei – teacher. All instructors are referred to as sensei
- 'Sensei ni rei' – 'bow to sensei'
- Seio otoshi – shoulder drop
- Shorinji Kan – Shorinji Kan Jiu Jitsu described in this book
- Side drop/kick up and drop – left and right falling technique designed to improve yoko ukemi (side falling)
- Simultaneous strikes – striking two vulnerable parts of the body at the same time
- Sports Jiu Jitsu – modern schools/styles of Jiu Jitsu focusing on competition and ground fighting. Less emphasis on self-defence and weapons defences
- Su dachi – standing with feet together

■ Suwari or seiza – kneeling position

## T

■ Tai otoshi – body drop

■ Tai sabaki – body positioning

■ Tani Otoshi – valley drop

■ Tapping out – hand movement on uke's torso indicating immediate submission

■ Tatami – mats to absorb the impact of your fall. Traditional tatami is made of straw

■ tate shiho gatame – lower four-quarters hold

■ Tori – the 'giver' of a technique. The person who performs themselves

■ Tsurikomi goshi – lifting pulling hip

## U

■ Ude garami – figure four arm entanglement – 3rd armlock

■ Ude gatame – straight armlock – 6th armlock

■ Uke – one who attacks or receives the technique. Training partner

■ Ukemi – breakfalling

■ Ukemi kata – breakfalling pattern

■ Uki goshi – floating hip

■ Ura hiza gatame – rear knee armlock

■ Ura kote gaeshi – rear hand twist

■ Ura kote – reverse twist – 2nd wristlock

■ Ushiro geri – rear kick

■ Ushiro ukemi – backwards fall

■ Ushiro yoko shiho gatame – reverse-side four-quarters hold

## W

■ Wakaza(u)shi – 'Short sword', used by the Samurai

■ Weakeners – technique (often to vulnerable part of the body) used to reduce uke or attacker's ability to resist main technique

■ Wrist locks – any counter-rotation or crush of the wrist joint

■ Wushu Monks – in Chinese, 'wu shu' means 'martial arts'. Traditionally, wushu was taught to Shaolin monks, who have recently toured the world demonstrating their skills

## Y

■ Yam(a)e – stop or halt

■ Yellow belt – 7th kyu

■ Yoi stance – attention – the 'ready stance'

■ Yoko Geri – side kick using either the side or the heel of the foot and aimed at the ribs, solar plexus, knees or shins

■ Yoko hiza gatame – side knee arm-lock

■ Yoko koto dori – side wrist trap

■ Yoko Shiho Gatame – side four-quarters hold

■ Yoko ude garami – side arm entanglement

■ Yoko ukemi – sideways fall

## Z

■ Zori – sandals

# INDEX

Page numbers with 'g' are glossary terms.

## A

aerobic warm-up exercises 170g
anaerobic warm-up exercises 170g
arm entanglements 72–3, 109–10
arm locks 56–7, 71–3, 88–9, 109–12, 127–33,
  159–60, 163–4
ashi sangaku garami 133, 170g
atemi 150, 170g
atemi waza 64–70, 89–91, 102–8, 126–7, 145
attacking 42, 79
awareness 43

## B

balance 38
basic mawashi geri 102
basic reaction warm up 30
belts, 21, 23–4, see also yellow belts; orange belts;
  green belts
blocks 35–7, 73–5, 89–91, 111, 170g
body drops 137–40, 150–1
body entanglements 160–1
body grabs 113
body locks 71, 159–60
body throws 136–7
bolt locks 57, 109
bottles 73–5, 118, 147–9, 158–63
bows 22
Brazilian Jiu Jitsu 15, 170g
British Ju Jitsu Association (GB) 170g
Bushido 15, 170g

## C

chest holds 145
control 41
coshes 118–19
countering 170g
cross blocks 111

## D

dachi 170g
dan grade 23–4, 170g
dangerous parts kata 170g

distance from attackers 145, 164
do 170g
dojo 21–2, 170g
drops 86–7, 137–43, 150–2, 170g

## E

ears 145–6
elbow locks 110–12, 163–4
embu 42, 123, 170–1g
entering body throws 136–7
etiquette 22–3

## F

faces 146, 159
falling 43, 85
finishing off 41, 96, 171g
fish hooks 171g
fists 107–8
floating hip throws 140–2
four-quarters holds 101–2, 143–4

## G

gedan ude garami 109–10, 171g
gi 21, 171g
grabs 75–7, 79–82, 113–16, 153–7
green belts 123–67, 171g
groins 146, 147
ground immobilisations 171g
groundwork 97–102, 164–7, 171g

## H

hair grabs 75–7
hands 105–7, 145–6
harai goshi 133–4, 147–8, 171g
heads 79, 153–7
  see also faces
hidari 171g
hiji gatame 110–12, 163–4, 171g
hip throws 92–3, 133–4, 135–6,
  140–2
hip wheels 95–6
history 14–15
hiza geri 104–5, 171g
holds 100–2, 143–5

## I

injuries 31
inside arm bolt locks 57
ippon seoi nage 93–4, 171g
irimi nage 136–7, 149–50, 171g

## J

Japanese 24, 26
Jigaro Kano 15, 171g
Jitsu 171g
Jitsu Foundation 23–4, 171g
Jiu Jitsu 171g
Jiu Jitsuka 171g
jodan ude garami 72–3, 160–1, 171g
joint locks 52–7
ju (Jiu) 171g
Judo 15, 171g
Judoka 171g

## K

kami shiho gatame 144, 172g
kannuki gatame 57, 109, 172g
Kano, Jigaro 15, 171g
kansetsu waza 52–7, 71–5, 88–91, 109–12, 127–33, 158, 172g
karada gatame 71, 159–60, 172g
karate 172g
kata 172g
kata gatame 100, 172g
kata guruma 172g
katana 15, 172g
katsugi gatame 61–2, 172g
keikogi 21, 172g
keza gatame 100, 172g
kiai 41–2, 172g
kiba dachi 23, 172g
kicks 102–4, 103–4, 126–7
kneecaps 146–7
knives 32, 117, 158–64
koshi guruma 95–6, 118–19, 172g
kosoto gake 61–2, 119, 164, 172g
kosoto gari 59–61, 172g
kote gaeshi 53–4, 172g
koto gatame 55–6, 172g
kujiki gatame 56–7, 172g
kung fu 172g
kuzushi 38–41, 98, 172g
kyu grades 23, 172g

## L

law 17, 18, 41
left-side training 42
lifting pulling hip throws 135–6, 150
locks 55–7, 61–2, 71, 109–12, 159–60, 163–4

## M

ma ai 145, 164, 172g
mae geri 103–4, 172g
mae ukemi 45–6, 172g
major inner reap from kick 112–13
major outer reaping throws 135–6
matae 172g
mawashi geri 102, 126–7, 172g
mawashi hiza geri 172–3g
mental strength 30
migi 173g
minor outer hook throws 61–2
minor outer reaping throws 59–61
mokusou 31, 173g
mons 23, 173g
movement 37, 46
movies 16
mune gatame 145, 173g
mushin 173g

## N

nage waza 58–62, 91–6, 112–16, 133–43, 147–52, 173g
ni dan 173g

## O

o goshi 92–3, 173g
o uchi gari 112–13, 173g
obi 173g
one-arm shoulder throws 93–4
orange belts 85–120, 173g
osaekomi waza 97–102, 143–5, 173g
osoto gari 58–9, 173g
otagi ni rei 23, 173g
over the belt 87, 173g
overarm grabs 113–15

## P

parries 35–7, 73–5, 173g
peg leg breakfall 173g
psychological preparation 159
punches 35–7

# R

ready stance 35, 159
reaps 58–9, 112–13
rei 22, 173g
reverse twists 54–5, 161–3
right-side training 42
rolls 46–9, 124–5
roundhouse cosh attack 118–19
roundhouse kicks 102, 104–5, 126–7

# S

safety 16–17, 20–2, 31–2, 64, 71, 146, 158–9, 160
Samurai 15, 24, 52, 64, 91, 173g
scarf holds 100
seiza *see* suwari
self-defence 17–19, 64–82, 102–17, 145–67, 173g
sensei 23, 173g
sensei ni rei 23, 173g
seoi otoshi 94–5, 173g
Shorinji Kan 173g
shoulders 61–2, 93–4, 94–5, 100
side drop/kick up and drop 87, 174g
side kicks 102–3
simultaneous strikes 108, 174g
slaps 146
sports Jiu Jitsu 174g
stances 35, 159
stomach, attacks to 163–4
stop 22
strangles 77–9
strength development 26, 30
stretching sequence 27–9
strikes 105–7, 108, 146
su dachi 23, 174g
suwari 23, 174g
sweeping hip throws 113–14, 133–4

# T

tai otoshi 137–40, 150–1, 174g
tai sabaki 174g
takedowns 98
tall person shoulder carry lock 61–2
tani otoshi 142–3, 152, 174g
tapping out 42, 53, 174g
tatami 22, 174g
tate shiho gatame 144, 174g
throws 58–62, 91–6, 98, 133–7, 140–2
tori 42, 174g

training 19, 20–1, 24–6, 42, 43, 82
tsurikomi goshi 135–6, 150, 174g

# U

ude garami 174g
ude gatame 174g
uke 42, 174g
ukemi 43, 49–51, 52, 85–7, 123–6, 174g
ukemi kata 46–9, 49–51, 123–4, 174g
uki goshi 140–2, 151–2, 174g
underarm grabs 70, 114–15, 116
uniform 21, 22
upper body arm entanglement 72–3
upper body entanglements 160–1
upper four-quarters holds 144
ura hiza gatame 174g
ura kote 54, 55, 161–3, 174g
ura kote gaeshi 174g
ushiro geri 126, 147, 174g
ushiro ukemi 43–4, 174g
ushiro yoko shiho gatame 143–4, 174g

# V

valley drops 142–3, 152

# W

wakaza(u)shi 174g
warming down 31
warming up 25–6
weakeners 37, 61, 174g
weapons 32, 117–20, 158–62
wrists 53–6, 79–82, 161–3, 174g
Wushu Monks 174g

# Y

yamae 22, 175g
yellow belts 35–83, 175g
yoi stance 35, 159, 175g
yoko geri 102–3, 146–7, 175g
yoko hiza gatame 175g
yoko koto dori 175g
yoko shiho gatame 101–2, 175g
yoko ude garami 175g
yoko ukemi 44–5, 175g

# Z

zori 175g